European sovereign-debt crisis

Long-term interest rates (secondary market yields of government bonds with maturities of close to ten years) of all eurozone countries except Estonia.[1] A yield being more than 4% higher compared to the lowest comparable yield among the Eurozone states, i.e. yields above 6% in September 2011, indicates that financial markets have serious doubts about credit-worthiness of the state.[1]

Note: Primary market yields are reported for Cyprus,[1] extracted from the government bond with longest maturity (CYGB 6.5%, 25 Aug 2021), which was issued in August 2011 with a maximum cut-off yield at 7.0%.[1] This mean that in market situations where the Cypriot government bond rate for comparable maturities exceeds the cut-off yield (which occurred throughout the entire period covered by the graph), this will not be noticed by the yield data for this type of bonds, having their maximum cut-off yield enforced. In order to asses "free market trade" values for Cypriot long-term government bond yields during 2010-2013, the secondary market yields of the Cypriot government bond with longest maturity but without a maximum cut-off yield enforced, is considered to be more accurate.[1] This bond, identified since January 2010 to be the (CYPGB 4.625%, EUR, 3 Feb 2020), had an average yield at 4.6% for January 2010[1] followed by a yield peak at 16.5% on 12 June 2012,[1] and was reported to be down at 11.5% on 17 May 2013.[1]

The Eurozone **crisis** (often referred to as the **Euro crisis**) is an ongoing crisis that has been affecting the countries of the Eurozone since late 2009. It is a combined sovereign debt crisis, a banking crisis and a growth and competitiveness crisis.[1]

The crisis made it difficult or impossible for some countries in the euro area to repay or re-finance their government debt without the assistance of third parties. Moreover, banks in the Eurozone are undercapitalized and have faced liquidity problems. Additionally, economic growth is slow in the whole of the Eurozone and is unequally distributed across the member states.[2]

In 1992, members of the European Union signed the Maastricht Treaty, under which they pledged to limit their deficit spending and debt levels. However, in the early 2000s, a number of EU member states were failing to stay within the confines of the Maastricht criteria and turned to securitising future government revenues to reduce their debts and/or deficits. Sovereigns sold rights to receive future cash flows, allowing governments to raise funds without violating debt and deficit targets, but sidestepping best practice and ignoring internationally agreed standards.[3] This allowed the sovereigns to mask their deficit and debt levels through a combination of techniques, including inconsistent accounting, off-balance-sheet transactions as well as the use of complex currency and credit derivatives structures.[5]

From late 2009, fears of a sovereign debt crisis developed among investors as a result of the rising private and government debt levels around the world together with a wave of downgrading of government debt in some European states. Causes of the crisis varied by country. In several countries, private debts arising from a property bubble were transferred to sovereign debt as a result of banking system bailouts and government responses to slowing economies post-bubble. In Greece, high public sector wage and pension commitments were connected to the debt increase.[6] The structure of the Eurozone as a monetary union (i.e., one currency) without fiscal union (e.g., different tax and public pension rules) contributed to the crisis and harmed the ability of European leaders to respond.[11][12] European banks own a significant amount of sovereign debt, such that concerns regarding the solvency of banking systems or sovereigns are negatively reinforcing.[13]

Concerns intensified in early 2010 and thereafter,[14][15] leading European nations to implement a series of financial support measures such as the European Financial Stability Facility (EFSF) and European Stability Mechanism (ESM).

Aside from all the political measures and bailout programmes being implemented to combat the Eurozone crisis, the European Central Bank (ECB) has also done its part by lowering interest rates and providing cheap loans of more than one trillion Euro to maintain money flows between European banks. On 6 September 2012, the ECB also calmed financial markets by announcing free unlimited support for all eurozone countries involved in a sovereign state bailout/precautionary programme from EFSF/ESM, through some yield lowering Outright Monetary Transactions (OMT).[16]

The crisis did not only introduce adverse economic effects for the worst hit countries, but also had a major political impact on the ruling governments in 8 out of 17 eurozone countries, leading to power shifts in Greece, Ireland, Italy, Portugal, Spain, Slovenia, Slovakia, and the Netherlands.

The Eurozone crisis has also become increasingly a social crisis for the most affected countries, with Greece and Spain having the highest unemployment rates in the currency area. Spain's unemployment was 26.9 percent in May 2013, while Greece's rate in March was 26.8 percent.[17]

Contents

Causes

Main article: Causes of the Eurozone crisis

The Eurozone crisis resulted from a combination of complex factors, including the globalisation of finance; easy credit conditions during the 2002–2008 period that encouraged high-risk lending and borrowing practices; the 2007–2012 global financial crisis; international trade imbalances; real-estate bubbles that have since burst; the 2008–2012 global recession; fiscal policy choices related to government revenues and expenses; and approaches used by nations to bail out troubled banking industries and private bondholders, assuming private debt burdens or socialising losses.

Evolution of the crisis

See also: 2000s European sovereign debt crisis timeline
See also: European debt crisis contagion

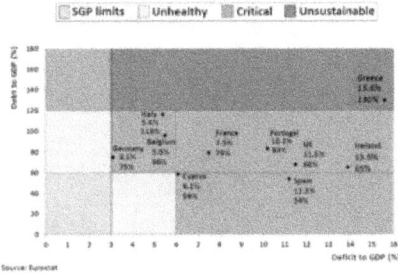

The 2009 annual budget deficit and public debt both relative to GDP, for selected European countries. In the eurozone, the following number of countries were: SGP-limit compliant (3), Unhealthy (1), Critical (12), and Unsustainable (1).

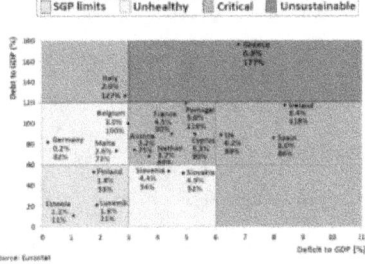

The 2012 annual budget deficit and public debt both relative to GDP, for all eurozone countries and UK. In the eurozone, the following number of countries were: SGP-limit compliant (3), Unhealthy (5), Critical (8), and Unsustainable (1).

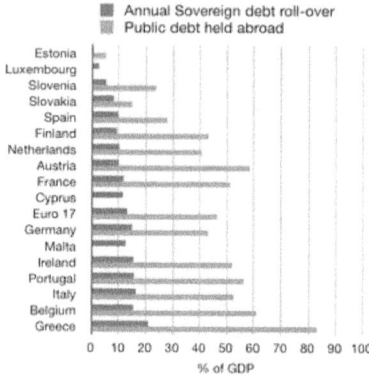

Debt profile of Eurozone countries

In the first few weeks of 2010, there was renewed anxiety about excessive national debt, with lenders demanding ever higher interest rates from several countries with higher debt levels, deficits and current account deficits. This in turn made it difficult for some governments to finance further budget deficits and service existing debt, particularly when economic growth rates were low, and when a high percentage of debt was in the hands of foreign creditors, as in the case of Greece and Portugal.[18] To fight the crisis some governments have focused on austerity measures (e.g., higher taxes and lower expenses) which has contributed to social unrest and significant debate among economists, many of whom advocate greater deficits when economies are struggling. Especially in countries where budget deficits and sovereign debts have increased sharply, a crisis of confidence has emerged with the widening of bond yield spreads and risk insurance on CDS between these countries and other EU member states, most importantly Germany.[18] By the end of 2011, Germany was estimated to have made more than €9 billion out of the crisis as investors flocked to safer but near zero interest rate German federal government bonds (*bunds*).[19] By July 2012 also the Netherlands, Austria and Finland benefited from zero or negative interest rates. Looking at short-term government bonds with a maturity of less than one year the list of beneficiaries also includes Belgium and France.[20] While Switzerland (and Denmark)[20] equally benefited from lower interest rates, the crisis also harmed its export sector due to a substantial influx of foreign capital and the resulting rise of the Swiss franc. In September 2011 the Swiss National Bank surprised currency traders by pledging that "it will no longer tolerate a euro-franc exchange rate below the minimum rate of 1.20 francs", effectively weakening the Swiss franc. This is the biggest Swiss intervention since 1978.[22]

Despite sovereign debt having risen substantially in only a few Eurozone countries, with the three most affected countries Greece, Ireland and Portugal collectively only accounting for 6% of the Eurozone's gross domestic product (GDP),[23] it has become a perceived problem for the area as a whole,[24] leading to speculation of further contagion of other European countries and a possible break-up of the Eurozone. In total, the debt crisis forced five out of 17 Eurozone countries to seek help from other nations by the end of 2012.

However, in Mid-2012, due to successful fiscal consolidation and implementation of structural reforms in the countries being most at risk and various policy measures taken by EU leaders and the ECB (see below), financial stability in the Eurozone has improved significantly and interest rates have steadily fallen. This has also greatly diminished contagion risk for other eurozone countries. As of October 2012 only 3 out of 17 eurozone countries, namely Greece, Portugal and Cyprus still battled with long term interest rates above 6%.[25] By early January 2013, successful sovereign debt auctions across the Eurozone but most importantly in Ireland, Spain, and Portugal, shows investors believe the ECB-backstop has worked.[26]

Greece

Main article: Greek government-debt crisis

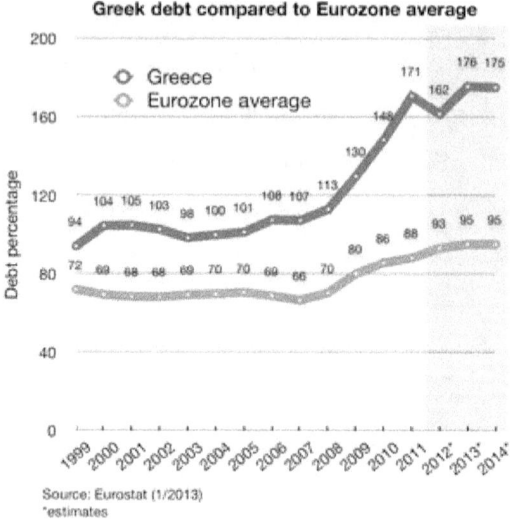

Greece's debt percentage since 1999 compared to the average of the eurozone.

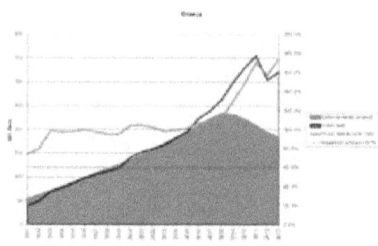

Public debt, gross domestic product (GDP), and public debt-to-GDP ratio

Graph based on "ameco" data from the European Commission

100,000 people protest against the austerity measures in front of parliament building in Athens, 29 May 2011

In the early mid-2000s, Greece's economy was one of the fastest growing in the eurozone and was associated with a large structural deficit.[22] As the world economy was hit by the global financial crisis in the late 2000s, Greece was hit especially hard because its main industries — shipping and tourism — were especially sensitive to changes in the business cycle. The government spent heavily to keep the economy functioning and the country's debt increased accordingly.

On 23 April 2010, the Greek government requested an initial loan of €45 billion from the EU and International Monetary Fund (IMF), to cover its financial needs for the remaining part of 2010.[26][27] A few days later Standard & Poor's slashed Greece's sovereign debt rating to BB+ or "junk" status amid fears of default,[28] in which case investors were liable to lose 30–50% of their money.[29] Stock markets worldwide and the euro currency declined in response to the downgrade.[31]

On 1 May 2010, the Greek government announced a series of austerity measures[33] to secure a three-year €110 billion loan.[33] This was met with great anger by the Greek public, leading to massive protests, riots and social unrest throughout Greece.[34] The Troika, a tripartite committee formed by the European Commission, the European Central Bank and the International Monetary Fund (EC, ECB and IMF), offered Greece a second bailout loan worth €130 billion in October 2011, but with the activation being conditional on implementation of further austerity measures and a debt restructure agreement. A bit surprisingly, the Greek prime minister George Papandreou first answered that call, by announcing a December 2011 referendum on the new bailout plan,[98][99] but had to back down amidst strong pressure from EU partners, who threatened to withhold an overdue €6 billion loan payment that Greece needed by mid-December.[100][101] On 10 November 2011 Papandreou resigned following an agreement with the New Democracy party and the Popular Orthodox Rally to appoint non-MP technocrat Lucas Papademos as new prime minister of an interim national union government, with responsibility for implementing the needed austerity measures to pave the way for the second bailout loan.[98][99]

All the implemented austerity measures, have helped Greece bring down its primary deficit – i.e. fiscal deficit before interest payments – from €24.7bn (10.6% of GDP) in 2009 to just €5.2bn (2.4% of GDP) in 2011,[30][31] but as a side-effect they also contributed to a worsening of the Greek recession, which began in October 2008 and only became worse in 2010 and 2011.[42] The Greek GDP had its worst decline in 2011 with −6.9%,[43] a year where the seasonal adjusted industrial output ended 28.4% lower than in 2005,[44][45] and with 111,000 Greek companies going bankrupt (27% higher than in 2010).[46][47] As a result, the seasonal adjusted unemployment rate grew from 7.5% in September 2008 to a record high of 27.2% in January 2013, while the Youth unemployment rate rose from 22.0% to as high as 59.3%.[48][49][50] Youth unemployment ratio hit 13 percent in 2011.[51][52] Overall the share of the population living at *"risk of poverty or social exclusion"* did not increase noteworthily during the first 2 years of the crisis. The figure was measured to 27.6% in 2009 and 27.7% in 2010 (only being slightly worse than the EU27-average at 23.4%),[53] but for 2011 the figure was now estimated to have risen sharply above 33%.[54] In February 2012, an IMF official negotiating Greek austerity measures admitted that excessive spending cuts were harming Greece.[49]

Some economic experts argue that the best option for Greece and the rest of the EU, would be to engineer an "orderly default", allowing Athens to withdraw simultaneously from the eurozone and reintroduce its national currency the drachma at a debased rate.[57][58] However, if Greece were to leave the euro, the economic and political consequences would be devastating. According to Japanese financial company Nomura an exit would lead to a 60% devaluation of the new drachma. Analysts at French bank BNP Paribas added that the fallout from a Greek exit would wipe 20% off Greece's GDP, increase Greece's debt-to-GDP ratio to over 200%, and send inflation soaring to 40%–50%.[57] Also UBS warned of hyperinflation, a bank run and even "military coups and possible civil war that could afflict a departing country".[58][59] Eurozone National Central Banks (NCBs) may lose up to €100bn in debt claims against the Greek national bank through the ECB's TARGET2 system. The Deutsche Bundesbank alone may have to write off €27bn.[60]

To prevent this from happening, the Troika (EC, IMF and ECB) eventually agreed in February 2012 to provide a second bailout package worth €130 billion,[61] conditional on the implementation of another harsh austerity package, reducing the Greek spendings with €3.3bn in 2012 and another €10bn in 2013 and 2014.[41] For the first time, the bailout deal also included a debt restructure agreement with the private holders of Greek government bonds (banks, insurers and investment funds), to "voluntarily" accept a bond swap with a 53.5% nominal write-off, partly in short-term EFSF notes, partly in new Greek bonds with lower interest rates and the maturity prolonged to 11–30 years (independently of the previous maturity).[62] It is the world's biggest debt restructuring deal ever done, affecting some €206 billion of Greek government bonds.[63] The debt write-off had a size of €107 billion, and caused the Greek debt level to fall from roughly €350bn to €240bn in March 2012, with the predicted debt burden now showing a more sustainable size equal to 117% of GDP by 2020,[64] somewhat lower than the target of 120.5% initially outlined in the signed Memorandum with the Troika.[41][65][66]

Critics such as the director of LSE's Hellenic Observatory argue that the billions of taxpayer euros are not saving Greece but financial institutions,[67] as "more than 80 percent of the rescue package is going to creditors—that is to say, to banks outside of Greece and to the ECB."[68] The shift in liabilities from European banks to European taxpayers has been staggering. One study found that the public debt of Greece to foreign governments, including debt to the EU/IMF loan facility and debt through the eurosystem, increased from €47.8bn to €180.5bn (+132,7bn) between January 2010 and September 2011,[69] while the combined exposure of foreign banks to (public and private) Greek entities was reduced from well over €200bn in 2009 to around €80bn (−120bn) by mid-February 2012.[70]

Mid May 2012 the crisis and impossibility to form a new government after elections and the possible victory by the anti-austerity axis led to new speculations Greece would have to leave the Eurozone shortly due.[71][72][73][74][75] This phenomenon became known as "Grexit" and started to govern international market behaviour.[76][77] However, the center-right's narrow victory in the 17 June election gave hope that Greece would honour its obligations and stay in the Euro-zone.[78]

Due to a delayed reform schedule and a worsened economic recession, the new government immediately asked the Troika to be granted an extended deadline from 2015 to 2017 before being required to restore the budget into a self-financed situation; which in effect was equal to a request of a third bailout package for 2015–16 worth €32.6bn of extra loans.[79][80] On 11 November 2012, facing a default by the end of November, the Greek parliament passed a new austerity package worth €18.8bn,[81] including a "labor market reform" and "midterm fiscal plan 2013–16".[82][83] In return, the Eurogroup agreed on the following day to lower interest rates and prolong debt maturities and to provide Greece with additional funds of around €10bn for a debt-buy-back programme. The latter allowed Greece to retire about half of the €62 billion in debt that Athens owes private creditors, thereby shaving roughly €20 billion off that debt. This should bring Greece's debt-to-GDP ratio down to 124% by 2020 and well below 110% two years later.[84] Without agreement the debt-to-GDP ratio would have risen to 188% in 2013.[85]

The Financial Times special report on the future of the European Union argues that the liberalization of labor markets has allowed Greece to narrow the cost-competitiveness gap with other southern eurozone countries by approximately 50 percent over the past two years.[84] This has been achieved primary through wage reductions, though businesses have reacted positively.[85] The opening of product and service markets, however, is proving tough because interest groups are slowing reforms.[85] The biggest challenge for Greece is to "overhaul the tax administration with less than 10 percent of annually assessed taxes paid."[85] However, Poul Thomsen, the IMF official who heads the bailout mission in Greece, stated that "in structural terms, Greece is more than halfway there."[85] In June 2013 Equity index provider MSCI Inc. reclassified Greece as an emerging market, citing failure to qualify on several criteria for market accessibility.[87]

Ireland

Main article: 2008–13 Irish financial crisis. Ireland's debt percentage compared to Eurozone average since 1995
Public debt, gross domestic product (GDP), and public debt-to-GDP ratio

Graph based on "ameco" data from the European Commission. The Irish government deficit compared to other European countries and the United States (2000–2014)[88]

The Irish sovereign debt crisis was not based on government over-spending, but from the state guaranteeing the six main Irish-based banks who had financed a property bubble. On 29 September 2008, Finance Minister Brian Lenihan, Jnr issued a two-year guarantee to the banks' depositors and bond-holders.[89] The guarantees were subsequently renewed for new deposits and bonds in a slightly different manner. In 2009, an National Asset Management Agency (NAMA), was created to acquire large property-related loans from the six banks at a market-related "long-term economic value".[89] Irish banks had lost an estimated 100 billion euros, much of it related to defaulted loans to property developers and homeowners made in the midst of the property bubble, which burst around 2007. The economy collapsed during 2008. Unemployment rose from 4% in 2006 to 14% by 2010, while the national budget went from a surplus in 2007 to a deficit of 32% GDP in 2010, the highest in the history of the eurozone, despite austerity measures.[89][90][91]

With Ireland's credit rating falling rapidly in the face of mounting estimates of the banking losses, guaranteed depositors and bondholders cashed in during 2009–10, and especially after August 2010. (The necessary funds were borrowed from the central bank.) With yields on Irish Government debt rising rapidly it was clear that the Government would have to seek assistance from the EU and IMF, resulting in a €67.5 billion "bailout" agreement of 29 November 2010.[92][93] Together with additional €17.5 billion coming from Ireland's own reserves and pensions, the government received €85 billion,[94] of which up to €34 billion was to be used to support the country's ailing financial sector (only about half of this was used in that way following stress tests conducted in 2011).[95] In return the government agreed to reduce its budget deficit to below three percent by 2015.[95] In April 2011, despite all the measures taken, Moody's downgraded the banks' debt to junk status.[96]

In July 2011 European leaders agreed to cut the interest rate that Ireland was paying on its EU/IMF bailout loan from around 6% to between 3.5% and 4% and to double the loan time to 15 years. The move was expected to save the country between 600–700 million euros per year.[97] On 14 September 2011, in a move to further ease Ireland's difficult financial situation, the European Commission announced it would cut the interest rate on its €22.5 billion loan coming from the European Financial Stability Mechanism, down to 2.59 per cent – which is the interest rate the EU itself pays to borrow from financial markets.[98]

The Euro Plus Monitor report from November 2011 attests to Ireland's vast progress in dealing with its financial crisis, expecting the country to stand on its own feet again and finance itself without any external support from the second half of 2012 onwards.[99] According to the Centre for Economics and Business Research Ireland's export-led recovery "will gradually pull its economy out of its trough". As a result of the improved economic outlook, the cost of 10-year government bonds, has already fallen substantially since its record high at 12% in mid July 2011 (see the graph "Long-term Interest Rates"). At 24 July 2012 it was down at a sustainable 6.3%,[100] and it is expected to fall even further to a level of only 4% by 2015.[99][1]

On 26 July 2012, for the first time since September 2010, Ireland was able to return to the financial markets selling over €5 billion in long-term government debt, with an interest rate of 5.9% for the 5-year bonds and 6.1% for the 8-year bonds at sale.[102]

By 2013 Ireland shouldered €41 billion (42%) of the total cost of the European banking crisis, or nearly €9,000 for each Irish citizen.[103]

Portugal

Main article: 2010–13 Portuguese financial crisis

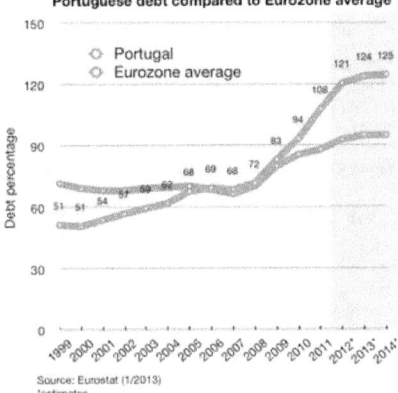

Portugal's debt percentage compared to Eurozone average since 1999

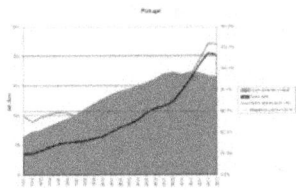

Public debt, gross domestic product (GDP), and public debt-to-GDP ratio

Graph based on "ameco" data from the European Commission

According to a report by the Diário de Notícias[100] Portugal had allowed considerable slippage in state-managed public works and inflated top management and head officer bonuses and wages in the period between the Carnation Revolution in 1974 and 2010. Persistent and lasting recruitment policies boosted the number of redundant public servants. Risky credit, public debt creation, and European structural and cohesion funds were mismanaged across almost four decades.[101] When the global crisis disrupted the markets and the world economy, together with the US credit crunch and the Eurozone crisis, Portugal was one of the first and most affected economies to succumb.

In the summer of 2010, Moody's Investors Service cut Portugal's sovereign bond rating,[104] which led to an increased pressure on Portuguese government bonds.[102]

In the first half of 2011, Portugal requested a €78 billion IMF-EU bailout package in a bid to stabilise its public finances.[106] These measures were put in place as a direct result of decades-long governmental overspending and an over bureaucratised civil service. After the bailout was announced, the Portuguese government headed by Pedro Passos Coelho managed to implement measures to improve the State's financial situation and the country started to be seen as moving on the right track. However, this also lead to a strong increase of the unemployment rate to over 15 percent in the second quarter 2012 and it is expected to rise even further in the near future.[109]

Portugal's debt was in September 2012 forecast by the Troika to peak at around 124% of GDP in 2014, followed by a firm downward trajectory after 2014. Previously the Troika had predicted it would peak at 118.5% of GDP in 2013, so the developments proved to be a bit worse than first anticipated, but the situation was described as fully sustainable and progressing well. As a result from the slightly worse economic circumstances, the country has been given one more year to reduce the budget deficit to a level below 3% of GDP, moving the target year from 2013 to 2014. The budget deficit for 2012 has been forecast to end at 5%. The recession in the economy is now also projected to last until 2013, with GDP declining 3% in 2012 and 1% in 2013; followed by a return to positive real growth in 2014.[118]

As part of the bailout programme, Portugal is required to regain complete access to financial markets starting from September 2013. The first step has been successfully completed on 3 October 2012, when the country managed to regain partial market access. Once Portugal regains complete access it is expected to benefit from interventions by the ECB, which announced support in the form of some yield-lowering bond purchases (OMTs),[120] to bring governmental interest rates down to sustainable levels. A peak for the Portuguese 10-year governmental interest rates happened on 30 January 2012, where it reached 17.3% after the rating agencies had cut the governments credit rating to "non-investment grade" (also referred to as "junk").[111] As of December 2012, it has been more than halved to only 7%.[112]

According to the Financial Times special report on the future of the European Union, the Portuguese government has "made progress in reforming labor legislation, cutting previously generous redundancy payments by more than half and freeing smaller employers from collective bargaining obligations, all components of Portugal's €78 billion bailout program."[86] Additionally, unit labor costs have fallen since 2009, working practices are liberalizing, and industrial licensing is being streamlined.[86] "But many reforms remain in the pipeline," the FT admits.[86]

Spain

See also: 2008–13 Spanish financial crisis

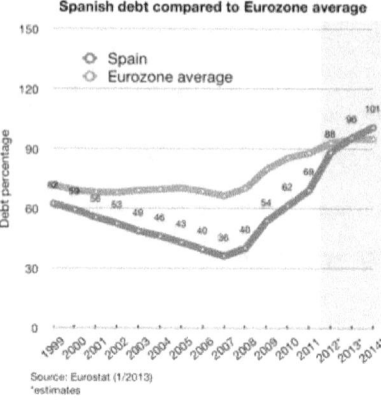

Spain's debt percentage compared to Eurozone average since 1999

Spain had a comparatively low debt level among advanced economies prior to the crisis.[113] Its public debt relative to GDP in 2010 was only 60%, more than 20 points less than Germany, France or the US, and more than 60 points less than Italy, Ireland or Greece.[114][115] Debt was largely avoided by the ballooning tax revenue from the housing bubble, which helped accommodate a decade of increased government spending without debt accumulation.[116] When the bubble burst, Spain spent large amounts of money on bank bailouts. In May 2012, Bankia received a 19 billion euro bailout,[117] on top of the previous 4.5 billion euros to prop up Bankia.[118] Questionable accounting methods disguised bank losses.[119] During September 2012, regulators indicated that Spanish banks required €59 billion (USD $77 billion) in additional capital to offset losses from real estate investments.[120]

The bank bailouts and the economic downturn increased the country's deficit and debt levels and led to a substantial downgrading of its credit rating. To build up trust in the financial markets, the government began to introduce austerity measures and it amended the Spanish Constitution in 2011 to require a balanced budget at both the national and regional level by 2020. The amendment states that public debt can not exceed 60% of GDP, though exceptions would be made in case of a natural catastrophe, economic recession or other emergencies.[121][122] As one of the largest eurozone economies (larger than Greece, Portugal and Ireland combined[123]) the condition of Spain's economy is of particular concern to international observers. Under pressure from the United States, the IMF, other European countries and the European Commission[124][125] the Spanish governments eventually succeeded in trimming the deficit from 11.2% of GDP in 2009 to an expected 5.4% in 2012.[126] Nevertheless, in June 2012, Spain became a prime concern for the Euro-zone[105] when interest on Spain's 10-year bonds reached the 7% level and it faced difficulty in accessing bond markets. This led the Eurogroup on 9 June 2012 to grant Spain a financial support package of up to €100 billion.[127] The funds will not go directly to Spanish banks, but be transferred to a government-owned Spanish fund responsible to conduct the needed bank recapitalisations (FROB), and thus it will be counted for as additional sovereign debt in Spain's national account.[128][129][130] An economic forecast in June 2012 highlighted the need for the arranged bank recapitalisation support package, as the outlook promised a negative growth rate of 1.7%, unemployment rising to 25%, and a continued declining trend for housing prices.[129] In September 2012 the ECB removed some of the pressure from Spain on financial markets, when it announced its "unlimited bond-buying plan", to be initiated if Spain would sign a new sovereign bailout package with EFSF/ESM.[131][132]

As of October 2012, the Troika (EC, ECB and IMF) is indeed in negotiations with Spain to establish an economic recovery program, which is required if the country should request a bailout package for the sovereign state from ESM. Reportedly Spain, in addition to the €100bn "bank recapitalisation" package arranged for in June 2012,[133] now also seeks sovereign financial support from a "Precautionary Conditioned Credit Line" (PCCL) package.[134] If Spain receives a PCCL package, irrespective to what extent it subsequently decides to draw on this established credit line, Spain would immediately qualify to receive "free" additional financial support from ECB, in the form of some unlimited yield-lowering bond purchases (OMT).[135][136] According to recent statements by the

Prime Minister, the country as of December 2012 still consider perhaps to request a PCCL sovereign bailout package in 2013, but only if developments at financial markets will promise Spain a significant financial advantage of doing so. As of 7 December 2012, the yield of 10-year government bonds had declined to 5.4%.[133]

According to the latest debt sustainability analysis published by the European Commission in October 2012, the fiscal outlook for Spain, if assuming the country will stick to the fiscal consolidation path and targets outlined by the country's current EDP programme, will result in a debt-to-GDP ratio reaching its maximum at 110% in 2018 – followed by a declining trend in subsequent years. In regards of the structural deficit the same outlook has promised, that it will gradually decline to comply with the maximum 0.5% level required by the Fiscal Compact in 2022/2027.[139]

Though Spain is suffering with 27 percent unemployment and an economy set to shrink by 1.4 percent in 2013, Mariano Rajoy's conservative government has pledged to speed up reforms, according to the Financial Times special report on the future of the European Union.[96] "Madrid is reviewing its labor market and pension reforms and has promised by the end of this year to liberalize its heavily regulated professions."[86] But Spain is benefiting from improved labor cost competitiveness.[96] "They have not lost export market share," says Eric Chaney, chief economist at Axa.[96] "If credit starts flowing again, Spain could surprise us."[86]

Cyprus
Main article: 2012–13 Cypriot financial crisis
The economy of the Republic of Cyprus was hit by several huge blows in and around 2012 including, amongst other things, the exposure of Cypriot banks to the Greek debt haircut, the downgrading of the Cypriot economy into junk status by international rating agencies and the inability of the government to refund its state expenses.[139]

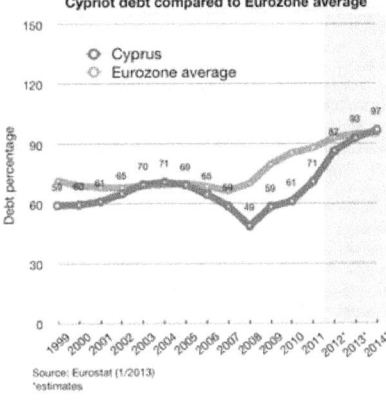

Cyprus's debt percentage compared to Eurozone average since 1999

In September 2011, the small island of Cyprus with 840,000 people was downgraded by all major credit rating agencies following the Evangelos Florakis Naval Base explosion in July and slow progress with fiscal and structural reforms. At the same time yields on its long-term bonds rose above 12%. Despite its low population and small economy Cyprus has a large off-shore banking industry that was shaken to its foundations during the financial turmoil. With a total nominal GDP of €19.5bn ($24bn[140]) the country was unable to stabilise its banks, which had amassed €22 billion of Greek private sector debt and were disproportionately hit by the haircut taken by creditors.[141][142][143]

The Cypriot Government was reported to have been requesting a bailout from the European Financial Stability Facility or the European Stability Mechanism on 25 June 2012, citing difficulties in supporting its banking sector from the exposure to the Greek debt haircut.[144] Representatives of the Troika (the European Commission, the International Monetary Fund, and the European Central Bank) arrived to the island in July for investigation over the financial problems of the country and submitted the terms of the bailout to the Cypriot government on 25 July.[145] The Cypriot government expressed disagreement over the bailout terms, and continued negotiation with Troika representatives concerning possible alterations to the terms throughout the following months.[148] On 20 November the government handed its counter-proposals to the Troika on the terms of the bailout,[147] with negotiations continuing. On 30 November it was reported that Troika and the Cypriot Government had agreed on the bailout terms with only the amount of money required for the bailout remaining to be agreed upon.[148] The bailout terms were made public on 30 November.[149] They include strong austerity measures, including cuts in civil service salaries, social benefits, allowances and pensions and increases in VAT, tobacco, alcohol and fuel taxes, taxes on lottery winnings, property, and higher public health care charges.[150]

In December 2012 a preliminary estimate indicated, that the needed overall bailout package should have a size of €17.5bn, comprising €10bn for bank recapitalisation and €6.0bn for refinancing maturing debt plus €1.5bn to cover budget deficits in 2013+2014+2015, which in total would have increased the Cypriot debt-to-GDP ratio to around 140%.[151] The final package negotiated and presented on 16 March 2013 however only entailed a €10bn support package,[152] financed partly by IMF (€1bn) and ESM (€9bn),[153] because it was possible to reach a fund saving agreement with the Cypriot authorities.[154] At first, the fund saving agreement comprised due to a specific request for this by the Cypriot finance minister, an unprecedented one-off levy of 6.7% for deposits up to €100.000 and 9.9% for higher deposits on all domestic bank accounts.[155] Following public outcry about neglect of the by EU law established Deposit Guarantee Scheme, the Eurozone finance ministers the next day however convinced Cypriot authorities instead to change the levy, into a higher 15.6% levy on deposits of above €100,000 ($129,600), while sparing depositors up to that level - in line with the EU law about existence of such a minimum deposit guarantee.[156] This revised deal was however rejected by the Cypriot parliament on 19 March 2013 with 36 votes against, 19 abstentions and one not present for the vote.[157]

When the final agreement was settled on 25 March, the idea of imposing any sort of deposit levy was dropped, as it was instead now possible to reach a mutual agreement with the Cypriot authorities accepting a direct closure of the most troubled Laiki Bank *(with remaining good assets and deposits below €100,000 being saved and transferred to Bank of Cyprus (BoC), while shareholder capital would be written off, and the uninsured deposits above €100,000 - along with other creditor claims - would be lost to the degree being decided by how much the receivership subsequently can recover from liquidation of the remaining bad assets)*, while as an extra safety measure, uninsured deposits above €100,000 in BoC will also remain frozen until a recapitalisation has been implemented *(with a possible imposed haircut if this is later deemed needed to reach the requirement for a 9% tier 1 capital ratio)*. The targeted closure of Laiki and recapitalisation plan for BoC helped significantly to reduce the needed loan amount for the overall bailout package, so that €10bn was still sufficient without need for imposing a general levy on bank deposits.[159]

The final conditions for activation of the bailout package was outlined by the Troika's MoU agreement, which was endorsed in full by the Cypriot House of Representatives on 30 April 2013, and include:[159][159]

> 1. Recapitalisation of the entire financial sector while accepting a closure of the Laiki bank,
> 2. Implementation of the anti-money laundering framework in Cypriot financial institutions,
> 3. Fiscal consolidation to help bring down the Cypriot governmental budget deficit,
> 4. Structural reforms to restore competitiveness and macroeconomic imbalances,
> 5. Privatization programme.

The Cypriot debt-to-GDP ratio is on this background now forecasted only to peak at 126% in 2015 and subsequently decline to 105% in 2020, and thus considered to remain within sustainable territory. The €10bn bailout comprise €4.1bn spend on debt liabilities (refinancing and amortization), 3.4bn to cover fiscal deficits, and €2.5bn for the bank recapitalization. These amounts will be paid to Cyprus through regular tranches from 13 May 2013 until 31 March 2016. According to the programme this will be sufficient, as Cyprus during the programme period in addition will:[159]

1. Receive €1.0bn extraordinary revenue from privatization of government assets.

2. Ensure an automatic roll-over of €1.0bn maturing Treasury Bills and €1.0bn of maturing bonds held by domestic creditors.
3. Bring down the funding need for bank recapitalization with €8.7bn, of which 0.4bn is a reinjection of future profits earned by the Cyprus Central Bank (injected in advance at the short term by selling its gold reserve), and €8.3bn origin from the bail-in of creditors in Laiki Bank and Bank of Cyprus.

Policy reactions

EU emergency measures

The table below provides an overview of the financial composition of all bailout programs being initiated for EU member states, since the Global Financial Crisis erupted in September 2008. EU member states outside the eurozone (marked with yellow in the table) have no access to the funds provided by EFSF/ESM, but can be covered with rescue loans from EU's Balance of Payments programme (BoP), IMF and bilateral loans (with an extra possible assistance from the Worldbank/EIB/EBRD if classified as a development country). Since October 2012, the ESM as a permanent new financial stability fund to cover any future potential bailout packages within the eurozone, has effectively replaced the now defunct GLF + EFSM + EFSF funds. Whenever pledged funds in a scheduled bailout program was not transferred in full, the table has noted this by writing *"Y out of X"*.

- v
- t
- e

The future of the European Union

 bioduniginla

May 24th, 2012

Current Location:

london, uk

by Natalie de Vallieres, Judith Stein, and Biodun Iginla, BBC News and The Economist

The choice

A limited version of federalism is a less miserable solution than the break-up of the euro

May 26th 2012 | from the print edition

•
•

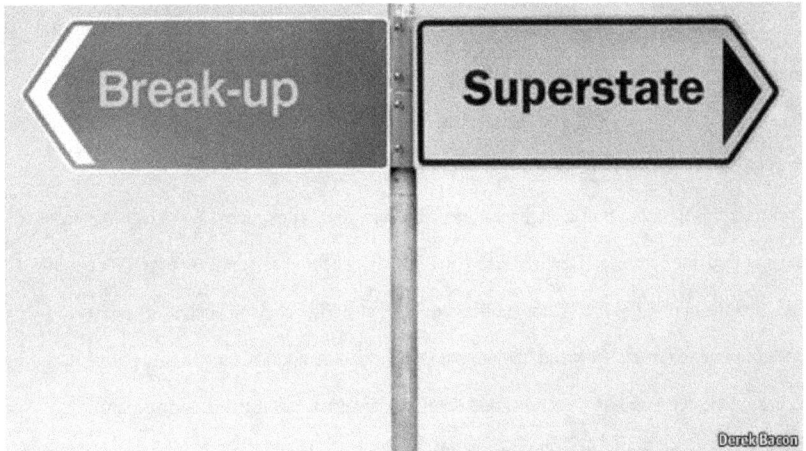

WHAT will become of the European Union? One road leads to the full break-up of the euro, with all its economic and political repercussions. The other involves an unprecedented transfer of wealth across Europe's borders and, in return, a corresponding surrender of sovereignty. Separate or superstate: those seem to be the alternatives now.

For two crisis-plagued years Europe's leaders have run away from this choice. They say that they want to keep the euro intact—except, perhaps, for Greece. But northern European creditors, led by Germany, will not pay out enough to assure the euro's survival, and southern European debtors increasingly resent foreigners telling them how to run their lives.

In this section

Reprints

This has become a test of over 60 years of European integration. Only if Europeans share a sense of common purpose will a grand deal to save the single currency be seen as legitimate. Only if it is legitimate can it last. Most of all, it is a test of Germany. Chancellor Angela Merkel maintains that the threat of the euro's failure is needed to keep wayward governments on the path of reform. But German brinkmanship is corroding the belief that the euro has a future, which raises the cost of a rescue and hastens the very collapse she says she wants to avoid. Ultimately, Europe's choice will be made in Berlin.

Last summer this newspaper argued that to break the euro zone's downward spiral required banks to be recapitalised, the European Central Bank (ECB) to stand behind solvent countries with unlimited support, and the curbing of the Teutonic obsession with austerity. Unfortunately, successive European rescue plans fell short and, though the ECB bought temporary relief by supplying banks with cheap, long-term cash in December and February, the crisis has festered and deepened.

In recent months we have concluded that, whether or not Greece stays in the euro, a rescue demands more. If it is to banish the spectre of a full break-up, the euro zone must draw on its joint resources by collectively standing behind its big banks and by issuing Eurobonds to share the burden of its debt. We set out the scheme's nuts and bolts below. It is unashamedly technocratic and limited, designed not to create the full superstate that critics (and we) fear. But it is plainly a move towards federalism—something that troubles many Europeans. It is a gamble, but time is running short. Rumours of bank runs around Europe's periphery have put savers and investors on alert (see article). The euro zone needs a plan.

Goodbye to all that

Is the euro really worth saving? Even the single currency's diehard backers now acknowledge that it was put together badly and run worse. Greece should never have been let in. France and Germany rode a coach and horses through the rules designed to prevent government borrowing getting out of hand. The high priests of euro-orthodoxy failed to grasp that, though Ireland and Spain kept to the euro's fiscal rules, they were vulnerable to a property bust or that Portugal and Italy were trapped by slow growth and declining competitiveness.

A break-up, many argue, would allow individual countries to restore control over monetary policy. A cheaper currency would help match wages with workers' productivity, for a while at least. Advocates of a break-up imagine an amicable split. Each government would decree that all domestic contracts— deposits and loans, prices and pay—should switch into a new currency. To prevent runs, banks, especially in weak economies, would shut over a weekend or limit withdrawals. To stop capital flight, governments would impose controls.

All good, except that the people who believe that countries would be better off without the euro gloss over the huge cost of getting there (see article). Even if this break-up were somehow executed flawlessly, banks and firms across the continent would topple because their domestic and foreign assets and liabilities would no longer match. A cascade of defaults and lawsuits would follow. Governments that run deficits would be forced to cut spending brutally or print cash.

And that is the optimistic scenario. More likely, a break-up would take place amid plunging global share prices, a flight to quality, runs on banks, and a collapse in output. Devaluation in weak economies and currency appreciation in strong ones would devastate rich-country producers. Capital controls are illegal in the EU and the break-up of the euro is outside the law, so the whole union would be cast into legal limbo. Some rich countries might take advantage of that to protect their producers by suspending the single market; they might try to deter economic migrants by restricting freedom of movement. Practically speaking, without the movement of goods, people or capital, little of the EU would remain.

The heirs of Schuman and Monnet would struggle to restore the Europe of 27 when it had been the cause of such mayhem—even if a euro-rump of strong countries emerged. Collapse would be a gift to anti-EU, anti-globalisation populists, like France's Marine Le Pen. There would be so many people to blame: Eurocrats, financiers, intransigent Germans, feckless Mediterraneans, foreigners of all kinds. As national politics turned ugly, European co-operation would break down. That is why this newspaper thinks willingly abandoning the euro is reckless. A rescue is preferable to a break-up.

A problem shared

But not just any rescue. Too much of the debate over how to save the euro puts the emphasis merely on a plan for growth. That would help, because growth makes debt more manageable and banks healthier. Mrs Merkel should have been more accommodating on this. But any realistic stimulus would be too modest to stem the crisis. The ECB could and should cut rates and begin quantitative easing, but official funds for investment are limited. More ambitious ways of boosting growth, such as the completion of a single European market for services, are sadly not even on the table.

In any case, the euro zone's troubles run too deep. Banks and their governments are propping each other up like Friday-night drunks. The ECB's support for the banks cannot prevent the weak economies of Spain, Portugal, Italy and Ireland from enfeebling their banks and governments. For as long as bond yields are high and growth is poor, sovereigns will face doubt about their capacity to service their debt and banks will see loans go bad. Yet that same uncertainty pushes up sovereign yields and stops bank lending, further inhibiting growth. Fear that the state might have to deal with a banking collapse makes government bonds riskier. Fear that the state could not cope makes a banking collapse more likely.

That is why we have reluctantly concluded that the nations in the euro zone must share their burdens. The logic is straightforward. The euro zone's problem is not the debt's size, but its fragmented structure. Taken as a whole, the stock of euro-zone public debt is 87% of GDP, compared with over

100% in America. Similarly, the banks are not too big for the continent as a whole, just for individual governments. To survive, Europe has to become more federal: the debate is how much more.

What's German for demoi?

A lot, according to some gung-ho federalists. For people like Germany's finance minister, Wolfgang Schäuble, the single currency was always a leg on the journey towards a fully integrated Europe. In exchange for paying up, they want to harmonise taxes and centralise political power with, say, an elected European Commission and new powers for the European Parliament. Voters will be scared into grudging acquiescence precisely because a euro collapse is so terrifying. In time, the new institutions will gain legitimacy because they will work and Europeans will begin to feel prosperous again (see article).

Yet to see the euro crisis as a chance to federalise the EU would be to misread people's appetite for integration. The wartime generation that saw the EU as a bulwark against strife is fading. For most Europeans, the outcome of the EU's most ambitious project, the euro, feels like misery. And there is no evidence that voters feel close to the EU. The Lisbon treaty and its precursor, the EU's aborted constitution, were together rejected in three out of six referendums; ten governments reneged on promises to put constitutional reform to the vote. The parliament is hopelessly remote.

Another version of the superstate is to accept that politics remains stubbornly national—and to increase the power of governments to police their neighbours. But that, too, has problems. As the euro crisis has shown, governments struggle to take collective decisions. The small countries of the euro zone fear that the big ones would hold too much sway. If Berlin pays the bills and tells the rest of Europe how to behave, it risks fostering destructive nationalist resentment against Germany. And like the other version of the superstate, it would strengthen the camp in Britain arguing for an exit—a problem not just for Britons but for all economically liberal Europeans.

The €50,300 ($64,000) question

That is why our rescue seeks to limit both the burden-sharing and the concession of sovereignty. Rather than building a federal system, it fills in two holes in the single currency's original design. The first is financial: the euro zone needs a region-wide system of bank supervision, recapitalisation, deposit insurance and regulation. The second is fiscal: euro-zone governments will be able to manage—and reduce—their fiscal burdens only with a limited mutualisation of debt. But in both cases the answer is not to transfer everything to the EU level.

Begin with the banks. Since the euro's creation, European integration has moved farthest in finance. Banks sprawl across national borders. German banks fuelled Spain's property boom, while their French peers funded Greece's borrowing.

The answer is to move the supervision and support of banks (or at least big ones) away from national regulators to European ones. At a minimum there must be a euro-zone-wide system of deposit insurance and oversight, with collective resources for the recapitalisation of endangered institutions and regional rules for the resolution of truly failed banks. A first step would be to use Europe's rescue funds to recapitalise weak banks, particularly in Spain. But a common system of deposit insurance needs to be rapidly set up.

These are big changes. Politicians will no longer be able to force their banks to support national firms or buy their government bonds. Banks will no longer be Spanish or German, but increasingly European. Make no mistake: this is integration. But it is limited to finance, a part of the economy where monetary union has already swept away national boundaries.

The fiscal integration can also be limited. Brussels need not take charge of tax and spending, nor need Eurobonds cover all government debts. All that is required is for overindebted countries to have access to money and for banks to have a "safe" euro-wide class of assets that is not tied to the fortunes of one country. The solution is a narrower Eurobond that mutualises a limited amount of debt for a limited amount of time. The best option is to build on an idea put forward by Germany's Council of Economic Experts, to mutualise the current debts of all euro-zone economies above 60%

of their GDP. Rather than issuing new national government bonds, everybody, from Germany (debt: 81% of GDP) to Italy (120%) would issue only these joint bonds until their national debts fell to the 60% threshold. The new mutualised-bond market, worth some €2.3 trillion, would be paid off over the next 25 years. Each country would pledge a specified tax (such as a VAT surcharge) to provide the cash.

So far Mrs Merkel has opposed all forms of mutualisation (and did so again this week—see Charlemagne). Under our scheme, Germany would pay more on a slug of its debt, subsidising riskier borrowers. But it is not a move to wholesale fiscal federalism. These joint bonds would not require intrusive federal fiscal oversight. Limited in scope and time, they do not fall foul of Germany's constitutional constraints. Indeed, they can be built from last autumn's beefed-up "six pack", which curbs excessive borrowing and deficits; and January's fiscal compact, which enshrines budget discipline in law and is now being ratified across the euro zone.

Even this more limited version of federalism is tricky. The single banking regulator might require a treaty change, which would be difficult when ten EU countries, including Britain, are not members of the euro. The treaty setting up Europe's bail-out fund would also have to be changed to allow money to be supplied directly to banks. Countries would have to find convincing ways to commit future governments to pay their share of the interest on the Eurobonds. Greece's debts so outweigh its economy that it would need a further rescue before entering any mutualisation scheme—though the sum involved is small on a continental scale.

So it is a long agenda; but it is more manageable than trying to redesign Brussels from the top down, and it is less costly than a break-up. Saving the euro is desirable and it is doable. One question remains: will Germans, Austrians and the Dutch feel enough solidarity with Italians, Spaniards, Portuguese and Irish to pay up? We believe that to do so is in their own interests. The time has come for Europe's leaders, and Mrs Merkel in particular, to make that case.

The **European sovereign debt crisis** (often referred to as the Eurozone **crisis**) is an ongoing financial crisis that has made it difficult or impossible for some countries in the euro area to repay or re-finance their government debt without the assistance of third parties.

In 1992, members of the European Union signed the Maastricht Treaty, under which they pledged to limit their deficit spending and debt levels. However, in the early 2000s, a number of EU member states were failing to stay within the confines of the Maastricht criteria and turned to securitising future government revenues to reduce their debts and/or deficits. Sovereigns sold rights to receive future cash flows, allowing governments to raise funds without violating debt and deficit targets, but sidestepping best practice and ignoring internationally agreed standards.[5] This allowed the sovereigns to mask their deficit and debt levels through a combination of techniques, including inconsistent accounting, off-balance-sheet transactions as well as the use of complex currency and credit derivatives structures.[6] Germany, for example, received €15.5 billion from the securitization of pension-related payments from Deutsche Telekom, Deutsche Post, and Deutsche Postbank in 2005–06, but guaranteed payments so investors bore only the risk of the German government's credit and the transactions were ultimately recorded in Europe's fiscal statistics as government borrowing, not asset sales.[7]

From late 2009, fears of a sovereign debt crisis developed among investors as a result of the rising private and government debt levels around the world together with a wave of downgrading of government debt in some European states. Causes of the crisis varied by country. In several countries, private debts arising from a property bubble were transferred to sovereign debt as a result of banking system bailouts and government responses to slowing economies post-bubble. In Greece, high public sector wage and pension commitments were connected to the debt increase.[10] The structure of the Eurozone as a monetary union (i.e., one currency) without fiscal union (e.g., different tax and public pension rules) contributed to the crisis and harmed the ability of European leaders to respond.[11][12] European banks own a significant amount of sovereign debt, such that concerns regarding the solvency of banking systems or sovereigns are negatively reinforcing.[13]

Concerns intensified in early 2010 and thereafter,[14][15] leading European nations to implement a series of financial support measures such as the European Financial Stability Facility (EFSF) and European Stability Mechanism (ESM).

Aside from all the political measures and bailout programmes being implemented to combat the European sovereign debt crisis, the European Central Bank (ECB) has also done its part by lowering interest rates and providing cheap loans of more than one trillion Euros to maintain money flows between European banks. On 6 September 2012, the ECB also calmed financial markets by announcing free unlimited support for all eurozone countries involved in a sovereign state bailout/precautionary programme from EFSF/ESM, through some yield lowering Outright Monetary Transactions (OMT).[15]

The crisis did not only introduce adverse economic effects for the worst hit countries, but also had a major political impact on the ruling governments in 8 out of 17 eurozone countries, leading to power shifts in Greece, Ireland, Italy, Portugal, Spain, Slovenia, Slovakia, and the Netherlands.

What really caused the eurozone crisis?

 bioduniginla

May 11th, 2012

Current Location:

london, uk

by Natalie de Vallieres, Biodun Iginla, Judith Stein, BBC News

World leaders probably spent more time worrying about the eurozone crisis than anything else in 2011.

And that was in the year that featured the Arab Spring, the Japanese tsunami and the death of Osama Bin Laden. What's more, 2012 looks set to be not much different. But as eurozone governments hammer out new rules to limit their borrowing, are they missing the point of the crisis?

Follow the path to find out.

Continue reading the main story

- The eurozone has agreed a new "fiscal compact"

- Eurozone leaders have agreed to a tough set of rules - insisted on by Germany - that will limit their governments' "structural" borrowing (that is, excluding any extra borrowing due to a recession) to just 0.5% of their economies' output each year. It will also limit their total borrowing to 3%. These rules are supposed to stop them accumulating too much debt, and make sure there won't be another financial crisis.

- But didn't they already agree to this back in the '90s?

- Hang on a minute. They agreed to exactly the same 3% borrowing limit back in 1997, when the euro was being set up. The "stability and growth pact" was insisted on by German finance minister Theo Waigel (centre of image). What happened?

- So who kept to the rules?

- Italy was the worst offender. It regularly broke the 3% annual borrowing limit. But actually Germany - along with Italy - was the first big country to break the 3% rule. After that, France followed. Of the big economies, only Spain kept its nose clean until the 2008 financial crisis; the Madrid government stayed within the 3% limit every year from the euro's creation in 1999 until 2007. Not only that - of the four, Spain's government also has the smallest debts relative to the size of its economy. Greece, by the way, is in a class of its own. It never stuck to the 3% target, but manipulated its borrowing statistics to look good, which allowed it to get into the euro in the first place. Its waywardness was uncovered two years ago.

- **3/9 Italy**
- Worst offender
- **5/9 Germany**
- First to break rules
- **6/9 France**
- Offender
- **9/9 Spain**
- Top of the Class
- But the markets have other ideas
- So surely Germany, France and Italy should be in trouble with all that reckless borrowing, while Spain should be reaping the rewards of its virtue? Well, no. Actually Germany is the "safe haven" - markets have been willing to lend to it at historically low interest rates since the crisis began. Spain on the other hand is seen by markets as almost as risky as Italy. So what gives?
- So what really caused the crisis?
- There *was* a big build-up of debts in Spain and Italy before 2008, but it had nothing to do with governments. Instead it was the private sector - companies and mortgage borrowers - who were taking out loans. Interest rates had fallen to unprecedented lows in southern European countries when they joined the euro. And that encouraged a debt-fuelled boom.

- Good news for Germany...
- All that debt helped finance more and more imports by Spain, Italy and even France. Meanwhile, Germany became an export power-house after the eurozone was set up in 1999, selling far more to the rest of the world (including southern Europeans) than it was buying as imports. That meant Germany was earning a lot of surplus cash on its exports. And guess what - most of that cash ended up being lent to southern Europe.
- ...bad news for southern Europe
- But debts are only part of the problem in Italy and Spain. During the boom years, wages rose and rose in the south (and in France). But German unions agreed to hold their wages steady. So Italian and Spanish workers now face a huge competitive price disadvantage. Indeed, this loss of competitiveness is the main reason why southern Europeans have been finding it so much harder to export than Germany.
- ...and a nasty dilemma
- So to recap, government borrowing - which has ballooned since the 2008 global financial crisis - had very little to do with creating the current eurozone crisis in the first place, especially in Spain (Greece's government is the big exception here). So even if governments don't break the borrowing rules this time, that won't necessarily stop a similar crisis from happening all over again. Spain and Italy are now facing nasty recessions, because no-one wants to spend. Companies and mortgage borrowers are too busy repaying their debts to spend more. Exports are uncompetitive. And now governments - whose borrowing has exploded since the 2008 financial crisis savaged their economies - have agreed to drastically cut their spending back as well. But...
- Cut spending...
- ...and you are pretty sure to deepen the recession. That probably means even more unemployment (already over 20% in Spain), which may push wages down to more

competitive levels - though history suggests this is very hard to do. Even so, lower wages will just make people's debts even harder to repay, meaning they are likely to cut their own spending even more, or stop repaying their debts. And lower wages may not even lead to a quick rise in exports, if all of your European export markets are in recession too. In any case, you can probably expect more strikes and protests, and more nervousness in financial markets about whether you really will stay in the euro.

- Don't cut spending...
- ...and you risk a financial collapse. The amount you borrow each year has exploded since 2008 due to economic stagnation and high unemployment. But your economy looks to be chronically uncompetitive within the euro. So markets are liable to lose confidence in you - they may fear your economy is simply too weak to support your ballooning debtload. Meanwhile, other European governments may not have enough money to bail you out, and the European Central Bank says its mandate doesn't allow it to. And if they won't lend to you, why would anyone else?

The Political Economy of the Euro-Zone Crisis

 bioduniginla

December 12th, 2010

Current Location:

cambridge, ma

http://www.allvoices.com/contributed-news/7598454-the-political-economy-of-the-eurozone-crisis

Sunday, 12 December 2010

Topic: eurozone crisis, bbc news

by Kenneth Anderson For The BBC's Biodun Iginla

In this week's Weekly Standard, Christopher Caldwell of the WS and FT has an essay specifically on the political economy of the euro-zone crisis, Euro Trashed: Europe's Rendezvous with Monetary Destiny. He notes that the European Union is built on a theory of successive crises, and that the euro was foreseen, perhaps intended, to provoke a crisis that would lead toward greater union; he quotes some of its founding fathers to that end. (I think he might have added the dialectical ideology that underlay that sentiment, but does not.):As we contemplate the macroeconomic storm that is now passing through Europe, we must bear in mind that this is a storm that the EU's promoters knew would come. The euro's designers understood Rahm Emanuel's philosophy about not letting a crisis go to waste. "Europe will be forged in crises," the European Community's founding father Jean Monnet wrote in his memoirs, "and it will be the sum of the solutions brought to these crises."

When the French statesman Jacques Delors laid out his plan for the euro in the late 1980s, he drew a clear trajectory: A common market had made possible a common currency. A common currency would make possible a common government.But how would that happen? After all, if a currency worked well within the existing political arrangements, there would be no reason for those arrangements ever to change. New institutions could result only from the currency's blowing up. Economic crisis would be the accidentally-on-purpose pretext for replacing a system based on parliamentary accountability with a system based on the whims of a handful of experts in Brussels. Europe's countries now face the choice of giving up either their newfangled money or their ancient national sovereignties. It is unclear which they will choose. Toward the end, the essay points out that although Greece is every bit as corrupt and profligate as the newspapers suggest, that was not the case with Spain, nor with Ireland, certainly not in the sense of Greece.

That is, Spain had quite good fiscal management and undertook measures that were thought quite strict at the time to protect its banks from the subprime crisis in the US, while many other European banks were as much a part of it as the US ones. True, Spain's economy has many structural problems - a sclerotic labor market for those in the protected sectors and, today, unemployment for everyone else. But the adjustment mechanisms by which democratic market societies overcome interest group recalcitrance - monetize the debt and let devaluation lower wages (behind the veil of money, as we Marxists like to say) - were not available to it, having joined the euro.

Spain was overcome by a one-size fits all monetary policy, which to overcome in a democratic society through internal fiscal and regulatory means alone would require superhuman willpower (and perhaps, in the regulatory arrangement of the EU and eurozone at this moment, could not be achieved in any case, on account of too many arbitrage avenues around internal controls, of the kind designed for the purpose of one-size fits all):The euro is an end-of-history currency. The late Dutch central banker Wim Duisenberg called it "the first currency that has not only severed its link to gold, but also its link to the nation state" ... Fans of the euro used to sell this post-national vision as a matter of hope. But today they are just as happy to sell it with fear. France's finance minister, Christine Lagarde, told a German newspaper recently that any wavering from European unity would be a "disaster." She said, "We need to go further towards a convergence of our economic policies."

One need not be particularly ideological to feel this way. One need only assume that, when economics speaks, politics must fall into line. Last summer, at the height of the Greek debt crisis, economists looked ahead to other problem countries and came to the uncomfortable conclusion that most of them had not been badly, incompetently, or corruptly run. There were exceptions, of course. Greece was corrupt by any historical or geographical standard. It would today be a basket case whether it had been using the euro, the drachma, or wampum. Ireland's ruling Fianna Fáil party certainly retained elements of the traditional cronyism that is Irish political culture's besetting sin, and which no one who has observed Boston politics for even a week will fail to recognize.But these are not the main problems the euro has wrought. The big damage has been in the private, not the public, sector. Politicians in Ireland may have got the occasional backhander from an unscrupulous property developer, but in the quantitative terms of balancing the budget, the Irish were model fiscal stewards until the property market collapsed.

Greece itself proved contagious partly because of the private-sector trade imbalances the euro created, which left French and German banks searching for debt to invest in. It was the Western private sector, as much as the Greek public sector, that rendered Greece too big to fail and put an end to the EU's no-bailouts rule.And then there is Spain, the other country whose rescue appears to be coming as inevitably as Christmas. Spain not only balanced its budget—it took precautions to keep its home lending sector from overheating. Unfortunately, even that was not enough to keep the artificially low real interest rates that the euro gave it from doing their damage. According to the Spanish macroeconomist Angel Ubide, Spain "probably should have been running fiscal surpluses of the order of 5–6 percent of GDP to offset the negative real interest rate its borrowers enjoyed."Well, as an economic matter, yes. Just as, as an economic matter, the United States should probably have been running surpluses to prepare for the wave of Baby Boom retirements that are fast approaching. But how would you have explained that to the Spanish people? Money burns a hole in the pocket of a democratic electorate. Voters hate reserves, surpluses, or any kind of money lying around. What do they call a 5–6 percent surplus? They call it "my money." Related Posts
No Related Post

"Politicians in Ireland may have got the occasional backhander from an unscrupulous property developer, but in the quantitative terms of balancing the budget, the Irish were model fiscal stewards until the property market collapsed."

This is in fact very wrong. Summary notes from "A Preliminary Report on The Sources of Ireland's Banking Crisis" commissioned by Brian Lenihan (Minister for Finance and a Teachta Dála (TD):

1. The response of supervisors to the build-up of risks, despite a few praiseworthy initiatives that came late in the process, was not hands-on or pre-emptive. To some degree, this was in tune with the times. The climate of regulation in advanced economies had swung towards reliance on market risk assessment. Domestically, moreover, there was a socio-political context in which it would have taken some courage to act more toughly in restraining bank credit. The weakness of supervision in Ireland contrasts sharply, however, with experience in those countries where supervisors, faced with evident risks, acted to stem the tide.

2. For a long time, Ireland's overall fiscal policy was considered to be exemplary because the country achieved fiscal surpluses every year from the mid-1990s to 2006, including the creation of a Pension Reserve Fund to make budget surpluses politically more acceptable.

3. However, the nominal budget figures mask an underlying deterioration in the fiscal situation after 1999. The cyclically-adjusted fiscal surplus was rather small during much of the last decade according to the data available at the time. As already mentioned, statistical tools to capture the full

impact of asset bubbles on tax revenue are not well developed, otherwise it would have become clearer much earlier that the structural, underlying fiscal balance was much less favourable than assumed at the time. The IMF estimates now that in 2007, when the headline budget was approximately in balance, the underlying, structural deficit (taking into account the large positive output gap and the effects of the asset price bubble) had deteriorated to 8 ¾ percent of potential GDP and amounted to 4 to 6 percent in the run-up to the crisis. The conclusion is that overall fiscal policies were pro-cyclical during most years up to, and including particularly, 2007 thus adding markedly to the overheating of the economy.

Therefore, the electorate of Ireland were the wrong model of "fiscal stewards" due to the ineffective management of the fiscal bottom line. Ireland's Exchequer did not have significant levels of money and regulators had rather poor counter-cyclical provisions. Regulators could have devised and implemented a decisive macro-prudential strategy that would dampened the property boom. But no, supervisory analysis and implementation fell short in these areas, macro-prudential risk, where the IMF, as noted in the Preliminary Report had hoped that a prudential framework would have proved valuable did not happen.

There is no question that a prudential framework could have been made to work sufficiently well to mitigate the impact of the credit/property cycle—instead we have a country dragged down and a journalist that is misinformed on the fiscal facts and scapegoating the "private sector" while praising the "public sector"–which instead needs maximum admonishment. 12.12.2010

at 2:15 am ESTDay Brea

It is a reassuring tale, and those worn down by the Wagnerian proportions of the euro saga (who isn't?) are eager to believe it. Unfortunately, the idea that the euro is yesterday's problem is a dangerous figment. In reality, Europe's leaders are sleepwalking through an economic wasteland.

In this section

- The sleepwalkers
- How to save Obama's second term
- Stand up for "Doing Business"
- The ultimate endorsement
- Lessons from cricket

Reprints

Someone call a somnambulance, quick

The euro-zone economy has just endured a sixth successive quarter of shrinking GDP. The malaise is spreading to core countries including Finland and the Netherlands, which both contracted in the first quarter. Retail sales are falling. Unemployment, above 12%, is a record—with more than one in four Spaniards out of work (see article). In spite of savage spending cuts, government deficits are persistent and high. The sum of government, household and company debt is still excessive. Banks are undercapitalised and international lenders worry about their as-yet-unrecognised losses. Although official interest rates are low, firms in southern Europe are suffering a cruel

credit

crunch. All this is causing economic hardship today and eating away at the prospects for growth tomorrow. The euro zone may not be about to collapse, but the calm in Brussels is not so much a sign of convalescence as of decay.

For everyone's sak

e

In the first few weeks of 2010, there was renewed anxiety about excessive national debt, with lenders demanding ever higher interest rates from several countries with higher debt levels, deficits and current account deficits. This in turn made it difficult for some governments to finance further budget deficits and service existing debt, particularly when economic growth rates were low, and when a high percentage of debt was in the hands of foreign creditors, as in the case of Greece and Portugal.[17] To fight the crisis some governments have focused on austerity measures (e.g., higher taxes and lower expenses) which has contributed to social unrest and significant debate among economists, many of whom advocate greater deficits when economies are struggling. Especially in countries where budget deficits and sovereign debts have increased sharply, a crisis of confidence has emerged with the widening of bond yield spreads and risk insurance on CDS between these countries and other EU member states, most importantly Germany.[18] By the end of 2011, Germany was estimated to have made more than €9 billion out of the crisis as investors flocked to safer but near zero interest rate German federal government bonds (*bunds*).[19] By July 2012 also the Netherlands, Austria and Finland benefited from zero or negative interest rates. Looking at short-term government bonds with a maturity of less than one year the list of beneficiaries also includes Belgium and France.[20] While Switzerland (and Denmark)[20] equally benefited from lower interest rates, the crisis also harmed its export sector due to a substantial influx of foreign capital and the resulting rise of the Swiss franc. In September 2011 the Swiss National Bank surprised currency traders by pledging that "it will no longer tolerate a euro-franc exchange rate below the minimum rate of 1.20 francs", effectively weakening the Swiss franc. This is the biggest Swiss intervention since 1978.[21]

Despite sovereign debt having risen substantially in only a few Eurozone countries, with the three most affected countries Greece, Ireland and Portugal collectively only accounting for 6% of the Eurozone's gross domestic product (GDP),[22] it has become a perceived problem for the area as a whole,[23] leading to speculation of further contagion of other European countries and a possible break-up of the Eurozone. In total, the debt crisis forced five out of 17 Eurozone countries to seek help from other nations by the end of 2012.

However, in Mid 2012, due to successful fiscal consolidation and implementation of structural reforms in the countries being most at risk and various policy measures taken by EU leaders and the ECB (see below), financial stability in the Eurozone has improved significantly and interest rates have steadily fallen. This has also greatly diminished contagion risk for other eurozone countries. As of October 2012 only 3 out of 17 eurozone countries, namely Greece, Portugal and Cyprus still battled with long term interest rates above 6%.[24] By early January 2013, successful sovereign debt auctions across the Eurozone but most importantly in Ireland, Spain, and Portugal, shows investors believe the ECB-backstop has worked.[25]

Greece

Main article: Greek government-debt crisis

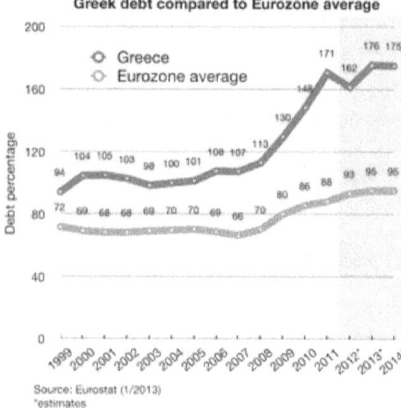

Source: Eurostat (1/2013)
*estimates

Greece's debt percentage since 1999 compared to the average of the eurozone.

100,000 people protest against the austerity measures in front of parliament building in Athens, 29 May 2011

In the early mid-2000s, Greece's economy was one of the fastest growing in the eurozone and was associated with a large structural deficit.[26] As the world economy was hit by the global financial crisis in the late 2000s, Greece was hit especially hard because its main industries — shipping and tourism — were especially sensitive to changes in the business cycle. The government spent heavily to keep the economy functioning and the country's debt increased accordingly.

On 23 April 2010, the Greek government requested an initial loan of €45 billion from the EU and International Monetary Fund (IMF), to cover its financial needs for the remaining part of 2010.[23][28] A few days later Standard & Poor's slashed Greece's sovereign debt rating to BB+ or "junk" status amid fears of default,[29] in which case investors were liable to lose 30–50% of their money.[29] Stock markets worldwide and the euro currency declined in response to the downgrade.[30]

On 1 May 2010, the Greek government announced a series of austerity measures[31] to secure a three-year €110 billion loan.[32] This was met with great anger by the Greek public, leading to massive protests, riots and social unrest throughout Greece.[33] The Troika (EC, ECB and IMF), offered Greece a second bailout loan worth €130 billion in October 2011, but with the activation being conditional on implementation of further austerity measures and a debt restructure agreement. A bit surprisingly, the Greek prime minister George Papandreou first answered that call, by announcing a December 2011 referendum on the new bailout plan,[34][35] but had to back down amidst strong pressure from EU partners, who threatened to withhold an overdue €6 billion loan payment that Greece needed by mid-December.[35][36] On 10 November 2011 Papandreou resigned following an agreement with the New Democracy party and the Popular Orthodox Rally to appoint non-MP technocrat Lucas Papademos as new prime minister of an interim national union government, with responsibility for implementing the needed austerity measures to pave the way for the second bailout loan.[37][38]

All the implemented austerity measures, have helped Greece bring down its primary deficit – i.e. fiscal deficit before interest payments – from €24.7bn (10.6% of GDP) in 2009 to just €5.2bn (2.4% of GDP) in 2011,[39][40] but as a side-effect they also contributed to a worsening of the Greek recession, which began in October 2008 and only became worse in 2010 and 2011.[41] The Greek GDP had its worst decline in 2011 with −6.9%,[42] a year where the seasonal adjusted industrial output ended 28.4% lower than in 2005,[43][44] and with 111,000 Greek companies going bankrupt (27% higher than in 2010).[45][46] As a result, the seasonal adjusted unemployment rate grew from 7.5% in September 2008 to a record high of 27.2% in January 2013, while the Youth unemployment rate rose from 22.0% to as high as 59.3%.[47][48][49] Youth unemployment ratio hit 13 percent in 2011.[50][51]

Overall the share of the population living at *"risk of poverty or social exclusion"* did not increase noteworthily during the first 2 years of the crisis. The figure was measured to 27.6% in 2009 and 27.7% in 2010 (only being slightly worse than the EU27-average at 23.4%),[52] but for 2011 the figure was now estimated to have risen sharply above 33%.[53] In February 2012, an IMF official negotiating Greek austerity measures admitted that excessive spending cuts were harming Greece.[9]

Some economic experts argue that the best option for Greece and the rest of the EU, would be to engineer an "orderly default", allowing Athens to withdraw simultaneously from the eurozone and reintroduce its national currency the drachma at a debased rate.[54][55] However, if Greece were to leave the euro, the economic and political consequences would be devastating. According to Japanese financial company Nomura an exit would lead to a 60% devaluation of the new drachma. Analysts at French bank BNP Paribas added that the fallout from a Greek exit would wipe 20% off Greece's GDP, increase Greece's debt-to-GDP ratio to over 200%, and send inflation soaring to 40%–50%.[56] Also UBS warned of hyperinflation, a bank run and even "military coups and possible civil war that could afflict a departing country".[57][58] Eurozone National Central Banks (NCBs) may lose up to €100bn in debt claims against the Greek national bank through the ECB's TARGET2 system. The Deutsche Bundesbank alone may have to write off €27bn.[59]

To prevent this from happening, the troika (EC, IMF and ECB) eventually agreed in February 2012 to provide a second bailout package worth €130 billion,[60] conditional on the implementation of another harsh austerity package, reducing the Greek spendings with €3.3bn in 2012 and another €10bn in 2013 and 2014.[60] For the first time, the bailout deal also included a debt restructure agreement with the private holders of Greek government bonds (banks, insurers and investment funds), to "voluntarily" accept a bond swap with a 53.5% nominal write-off, partly in short-term

EFSF notes, partly in new Greek bonds with lower interest rates and the maturity prolonged to 11–30 years (independently of the previous maturity).[61] It is the world's biggest debt restructuring deal ever done, affecting some €206 billion of Greek government bonds.[62] The debt write-off had a size of €107 billion, and caused the Greek debt level to fall from roughly €350bn to €240bn in March 2012, with the predicted debt burden now showing a more sustainable size equal to 117% of GDP by 2020,[63] somewhat lower than the target of 120.5% initially outlined in the signed Memorandum with the Troika.[49][64][65]

Critics such as the director of LSE's Hellenic Observatory argue that the billions of taxpayer euros are not saving Greece but financial institutions,[66] as "more than 80 percent of the rescue package is going to creditors—that is to say, to banks outside of Greece and to the ECB."[67] The shift in liabilities from European banks to European taxpayers has been staggering. One study found that the public debt of Greece to foreign governments, including debt to the EU/IMF loan facility and debt through the eurosystem, increased from €47.8bn to €180.5bn (+132,7bn) between January 2010 and September 2011,[68] while the combined exposure of foreign banks to (public and private) Greek entities was reduced from well over €200bn in 2009 to around €80bn (−120bn) by mid-February 2012.[69]

Mid May 2012 the crisis and impossibility to form a new government after elections and the possible victory by the anti-austerity axis led to new speculations Greece would have to leave the Eurozone shortly due.[70][71][72][73][74] This phenomenon became known as "Grexit" and started to govern international market behaviour.[75][76] However, the center-right's narrow victory in the 17 June election gave hope that Greece would honour its obligations and stay in the Euro-zone.[77]

Due to a delayed reform schedule and a worsened economic recession, the new government immediately asked the Troika to be granted an extended deadline from 2015 to 2017 before being required to restore the budget into a self-financed situation; which in effect was equal to a request of a third bailout package for 2015–16 worth €32.6bn of extra loans.[78][79] On 11 November 2012, facing a default by the end of November, the Greek parliament passed a new austerity package worth €18.8bn,[80] including a "labor market reform" and "midterm fiscal plan 2013–16".[81][82] In return, the Eurogroup agreed on the following day to lower interest rates and prolong debt maturities and to provide Greece with additional funds of around €10bn for a debt-buy-back programme. The latter allowed Greece to retire about half of the €62 billion in debt that Athens owes private creditors, thereby shaving roughly €20 billion off that debt. This should bring Greece's debt-to-GDP ratio down to 124% by 2020 and well below 110% two years later.[83] Without agreement the debt-to-GDP ratio would have risen to 188% in 2013.[84]

The Financial Times special report on the future of the European Union argues that the liberalization of labor markets has allowed Greece to narrow the cost-competitiveness gap with other southern eurozone countries by approximately 50 percent over the past two years.[85] This has been achieved primary through wage reductions, though businesses have reacted positively.[85] The opening of product and service markets, however, is proving tough because interest groups are slowing reforms.[85] The biggest challenge for Greece is to "overhaul the tax administration with less than 10 percent of annually assessed taxes paid."[85] However, Poul Thomsen, the IMF official who heads the bailout mission in Greece, stated that "in structural terms, Greece is more than halfway there."[85]

Europe's leaders must shake themselves out of their lethargy. They must grasp that if they do not act, the euro zone faces stagnation or break-up—possibly both.

After years of crisis, the to-do list is clear. The urgent task is to sever the ties between banks and governments too feeble to support them. That was the aim of the banking union agreed on last year. But, as the pressure has eased, the union has become ensnared in technicalities and a fundamental argument about how much historic bank debt, if any, should be dumped on it—how much, in other words, Germans, Finns and Dutch should bear the burden of other people's mistakes. This delay is highly damaging. Europe's banks need funds by whatever means. America has recovered before Europe not just because it has been less austere, but also because it rapidly sorted out its banks so that they could lend again (see Charlemagne).

In addition, the euro zone needs growth-boosting reform. The EU should extend the single market further into services. Instead of thinking up red lines, it should pursue a free-trade agreement on offer from the United States, its biggest

trading

partner. And it should ease austerity by slowing the pace of budget cuts and using cash from the core euro zone to pay for schemes to boost youth employment and investment in small and medium-sized firms in the periphery.

Clearly, the reason for today's inaction is not a shortage of things to do, but a shortage of the will to do them. This hiatus is partly caused by elections due in September in Germany, the prime mover in almost any European policy these days. But there is a deeper reason, too. Across Europe voters have grown resentful of both their own politicians and the EU. In France the president, François Hollande, is paralysed by scandal and a dismal approval rating of 24%, another record (see article). A recent

survey

by the Pew Research Centre found that the share of French voters who say that they look favourably on the EU has fallen from 60% in 2012 to 41% now, less even than in Eurosceptic Britain. Italy is mired in recession, yet it cannot seem to muster a coherent political platform for change. At the same time, voters want to keep the single currency: 70% of them still support the euro in Greece, which has suffered more in the crisis than any other country. Over the past few years crunch votes in Greece, Ireland, Portugal, Spain and the Netherlands have repeatedly backed staying inside the euro zone.

This is a recipe for inaction. On the one hand, voters want the euro zone to stay together. On the other, they will not back the difficult reforms needed to pull it out of the crisis.

Time was when the bond markets would force politicians to face up to this contradiction. It was the threat of financial panic that kept euro-zone leaders up until dawn hammering out rescue deals and promises of reform. But the financial markets have been anaesthetised ever since Mario Draghi, the president of the European Central Bank (ECB), promised to "do whatever it takes" to protect the euro zone from collapse. Speculators know that to bet against the single currency would be to take on the theoretically infinite balance-sheet of the ECB—and that, at least at first, would mean heavy losses.

Alarm bells

Mr Draghi was right to buy the euro zone time. He was also right to furnish the ECB with the tools to tamp down speculation. The trouble is that the politicians are squandering the chance for orderly reform. Optimists say that everything will be just fine after Germany's election, when its leaders will have a mandate for euro-zone reform. But German reluctance either to lead or to pay for the rest of Europe runs deeper than that. Besides, Mr Hollande's woes mean that the Franco-German relationship, always central to the evolution of Europe, has seized up.

And if euro-zone leaders stumble on? Like Japan, Europe will be under a shadow for years to come. The cost will be measured in disillusion, blighted communities and wasted lives. Unlike Japan, though, the euro zone is not cohesive. For as long as stagnation and recession tear at democracy, the euro zone risks a fatal popular rejection. If the sleepwalkers care about their currency and their people, they need to wake up.

Italy at heart of crisis as borrowing costs climb

- by Natalie de Vallieres and Biodun Iginla, BBC News

Italy's borrowing costs jumped to record levels Friday, underlining its vulnerability at the heart of the euro zone debt crisis and skepticism about whether the struggling government of Prime Minister Silvio Berlusconi can deliver vital reforms.

The 6.06 percent yield paid at an auction of 10-year bonds was the highest since the launch of the euro, and not far from the level reached before the European Central Bank intervened in August to cap Rome's borrowing costs by buying Italian debt.

Italy, the euro zone's third largest economy, is again at the center of the debt crisis, as fears grow that its borrowing costs could hit levels that overwhelm the capacity of the bloc to provide support amid chronic political instability in Rome.

In a speech in Rome, Berlusconi insisted that Italy would meet its target of balancing the budget by 2013.

Tainted by scandal and repeatedly at odds with his coalition allies, Berlusconi has promised European partners a package of measures to spur Italy's stagnant economy and cut its towering public debt, but has failed to convince markets made skeptical by his repeated failure to deliver reforms.

European leaders welcomed a letter of intent on reforms that he delivered to their summit last Wednesday, but emphasized that the measures must now be implemented.

"The interest rates that they are paying are punitive," said Monument Securities strategist Marc Oswald. "Italy … is still the 'bete noire' of the whole euro zone problem."

"They are still going to carry on having to pay higher yields unless they come up with reform plans and implement them. But anyone who expresses an optimistic opinion about that is probably looking through rose-tinted glasses," he added.

EXASPERATION

France and Germany have expressed open exasperation at a succession of unfulfilled reform promises by Berlusconi, and fear the crisis in Italy could spark a wider emergency that would threaten the very existence of the single currency.

Even if a weakened government manages to pass the promised reforms, most will not come into force until mid-2012. Markets are unlikely to remain patient for so long.

In his speech Berlusconi took aim at the euro, calling it a "strange" currency.

"There is an attack on the euro which as a currency has convinced no-one, because it belongs to more than one country but does not have a bank of reference and guarantee," he said, referring to reluctance by Germany and other countries to allow the European Central Bank to be used as a lender of last resort.

He later issued a statement saying his words had been interpreted in a "malicious and distorted" way.

"The euro is our currency, our flag. It is precisely to defend the euro from speculative attacks that Italy is making great sacrifices," the statement said.

Berlusconi, who is facing two court cases for accusations of fraud and one for allegedly having sex with an underage prostitute, complained that he faced 37 judicial hearings between now and mid-January. He says leftist magistrates are persecuting him in an attempt to undermine democracy.

Speaking after Wednesday's summit, French President Nicolas Sarkozy addressed fears that the crisis could spread to Italy.

"If we had allowed Greece to fall, and the speculation shifted on to attack Italy, the markets would then have said we will allow Italy to fall too, and that would be the end of the euro," he said in a television interview.

As Italy sinks deeper into the debt crisis, tensions in the government have grown sharply, prompting widespread speculation in the press and even Berlusconi's party that the government will fall, leading to an election in 2012, a year early.

"COALITION IS SOLID"

Berlusconi, whose ratings have been torpedoed by a mix of scandal and economic and political problems, rejected speculation that he might be forced into an early election.

He said his alliance remained solid with the pro-devolution Northern League party, whose leader Umberto Bossi has expressed open skepticism about the survival of the coalition.

"There is an absolute need for political stability and Bossi thinks exactly the same way I do. The pact we have with the League has never been up for discussion," Berlusconi said.

"No credible political alternative exists."

This week the League rejected plans to raise the pension age to 67, leading to tense late-night talks before a compromise was reached in time to take to the summit in Brussels.

The proposals, including an increase in the pension age, rules making it easier to lay off staff and provisions to place civil servants in special redundancy schemes, have raised fierce opposition from unions and skepticism about whether they will ever be implemented.

In Italy's increasingly murky politics, there has been speculation that the package is part of a deal between Berlusconi and Bossi to take the government to the end of the year before triggering an election in the spring.

Friday, Berlusconi dismissed such suggestions and said an election campaign in the middle of the crisis would be "very seriously damaging to Italy."

EVEN by the euro zone's undemanding standards, a summit deal that survived less than a week is lamentable. Early on October 27th Angela Merkel, the German chancellor, and Nicolas Sarkozy, the French president, hailed a "comprehensive package" to save the euro. Yet by the time *The Economist* went to press, their plans were in tatters. Greece's prime minister, George Papandreou, looked doomed, rejected by some of his ministers, many in his party—and, possibly, most of his country.

The shallowness of the summit's achievements has been brutally exposed. Instead of settling into a period of calm, markets were thrown into new turmoil (see article). One way or another, the euro is destined for an unavoidable test of popular support. Unless the euro zone's leaders shape up, this is an encounter their currency may well lose.

Heed the messenger

Mr Papandreou was in part the author of his own misfortune. Seeking the backing of the Greek people in a referendum, he was immediately condemned in the capitals of Europe as a fool or a traitor. Why had he wrecked all their good work? How dare he bring disaster on the rest of the euro zone when it had so generously bailed out his scapegrace of a country? A furious Mr Sarkozy and Mrs Merkel summoned him for a dressing-down on the fringes of the G20 summit in Cannes. Mr Sarkozy's hopes that this gathering might set the stage for generous emerging-market investment to support the euro were already faint. They now look impossible.

There is no disputing that Mr Papandreou, in spectacularly chaotic style, has left the euro zone racked by uncertainty. His referendum now seems unlikely to take place. Perhaps Pasok, his party, will enter a government of national unity with New Democracy, the opposition, headed by a technocrat. Perhaps there will be an election. Perhaps even these plans will fall apart, just as the last did (see article). All the while, the clock is ticking: within a month or so, Greece must receive fresh funds from the IMF and its European rescuers—or messily default.

Mr Papandreou has created an almighty mess, but he is better cast as the messenger than the villain. He was not to blame for the summit's shortcomings. The spreads between Italian and German government debt had begun to widen well before Mr Papandreou dropped his bombshell. If the euro zone had put a credible firewall around the government bonds of Italy and other troubled euro countries, a Greek default would not now be threatening contagion. Stable sovereign borrowers would have helped to safeguard Europe's banks, and a decent plan to strengthen the weakest banks would have secured the door. But last week's summit deal—concocting a jerry-built firewall and asking the banks to boost their capital ratios by June next year—was not up to scratch. No wonder the markets took fright only days later.

At one level, Mr Papandreou does not deserve blame even for seeking a mandate on the summit's main achievement (though he must now be ruing his decision). Although the proposal to write down the face value of privately held Greek-government debt by 50% would be substantial and welcome, Greece's stock of debt would, even on best assumptions, still add up to 120% of GDP by 2020. All the while, the Greek people would be living with austerity.

Hence Mr Papandreou's most important message. Until now the euro crisis has chiefly been about pressure from the markets. But a country's finances are not defined by markets alone. Rather the limits of solvency are tested by people's willingness to accept tax rises and spending cuts. A government runs out of political capital long before it runs out of things to tax. In the end, won't pay matters more than can't pay.

Greece is farther down this road than any other member of the euro zone—even though other countries such as Portugal and Ireland have already seen their governments toppled and Spain is about to follow suit. Beset by rebels in his own party, by a hostile media and by strikes and protests, Mr Papandreou concluded that he would find it hard to impose the austerity being asked of Greece. Every quarter the EU, the IMF and the European Central Bank (ECB) scrutinise Greece before releasing the next chunk of money. With nowhere to hide, he decided to appeal over the heads of his opponents to the people.

Greece's next government, whatever its composition, cannot escape the growing resentment of the country's political class. A growing but still small contingent of Greeks wants to defy the EU's treaties and quit the euro altogether. Fully 60% reject the summit deal. But Greek withdrawal still looks like a terrible mistake. Depositors would rush to pull their money out of Greek banks to protect their savings from being converted into new drachma. Greek firms would be bankrupted by their euro debts. The gain in competitiveness from devaluation would be transient if, as is likely, wages inflated along with prices. Even Greece's EU membership would be in doubt.

What to do?

Greece's government must wisely spend what scant political capital it may have. Above all, the economy needs to grow. Despite their anger, 70% of Greeks say they want to remain in the euro, but their tolerance for austerity has limits. The government must devote less effort to growth-destroying tax rises and instead undertake growth-promoting structural reforms. It will have to begin facing down public-sector unions and enforcing barely implemented reforms. Mr Papandreou's government consistently took the easy way out.

The euro zone's emphasis on austerity rather than structural reforms has aggravated Greece's political woes. Instead it should favour medium-term fiscal consolidation. The creditor nations could boost domestic demand, to provide a bigger market for debtors' exports. Most of all, they should dispel the threat of contagion by putting the ECB's balance-sheet behind the debt of solvent governments, like Italy and Spain. Throughout this crisis, creditors—particularly Germany—have worried about being too soft on the euro zone's weaklings, for fear that they would go slow on reform. Mr Papandreou has shown that they also need to worry about being too austere.

EVEN in a grouping as fractious as the euro zone, tonight's falling-out was remarkable. Jean-Claude Juncker, who presides over the zone's finance ministers, lashed out at the many figures who have more or less openly threatened Greece with expulsion from the euro if it does not abide by its programme of economic reforms and austerity measures.

With Greece in deep political turmoil (some are even talking apocalyptically of civil war) after voters backed an incoherent constellation of anti-austerity parties, European central bankers and finance ministers have been warning it that its departure from the euro is inevitable if it does not abide by the terms of its bail-out.

One of the bluntest warnings came from the president of the European Commission, José Manuel Barroso, who told Italy's SkyTG24: "If a member of a club does not respect the rules, it's better that it leaves the club—and this is true for any organisation or institution or any project."

Mr Juncker, who is also Luxembourg's prime minister, was having none of this. Speaking at the official press conference at the end of a five-hour meeting of euro-zone finance ministers (the "euro group"), he let rip:

I made it perfectly clear that nobody was mentioning an exit of Greece from the euro area. I am strongly against. We are 17 member-states being co-owners of our common currency. I don't envisage, not even for one second, Greece leaving the euro area. This is nonsense, this is propaganda. We have to respect Greek democracy. I'm against this way of dealing with Greece, [which consists] in provoking the Greek public opinion and giving advice and indications to the Greek sovereign. Greece has voted, we have to take into account the result. We do hope that a government will be formed in the next coming days or weeks and then we have to deal with that government. We don't have to lecture Greece.

But the Greek public, the Greek citizens, have to know that we agreed on a programme and this programme has to be implemented. But I don't like the way of dealing with Greece, those that are threatening Greece day after day. This is not the way of dealing with partners, colleagues and friends and citizens in the European Union.

Mr Juncker's comments are all the more striking given that, just next to him, Olli Rehn, the Finnish commissioner for economic and monetary affairs, delivered the now-standard warning to Greece about the danger of rejecting the bail-out conditions set by the EU and IMF:

The EU-IMF programme is a very substantial expression of solidarity and support for Greece by the other 16 euro-area member-states. It is in fact a solidarity pact between the other 16 euro-area member-states and Greece, between the 16 parliaments and the Greek parliament. This is what Europe is about. But solidarity is a two-way street. It is a fact that calls for respect of commitments both by the 16 euro-area member-states and also by Greece and its government and parliament. Without a Greek commitment this solidarity pact won't work, and this is the responsibility of Greek politicians in this very critical juncture. Hence the future of Greece and the welfare of its citizens lie more than ever on the shoulders of Greek politicians to keep their part of the solidarity pact.

One might conclude that Mr Juncker and Mr Rehn were playing good-cop, bad-cop with Greece. More likely, their comments reflect two factors. The first is that Mr Juncker feels free to speak out because he will soon step down as the group's president (he recently criticised the behaviour of France and Germany). The second is that the euro zone is deeply divided over how to deal with the insubordination of Greek voters—and whether it can withstand the shock of a Greek departure from the currency union. Mr Juncker left open the possibility of renegotiating the Greek package "in exceptional circumstances", but only once a new Greek government had been formed and had accepted the reform programme.

Officials such as Mr Rehn argue that, two years into the debt crisis, the euro zone is more prepared than ever for what is now known as "Grexit", having raised its firewalls and started recapitalising vulnerable banks. The manifest fear in the markets, though, suggests that investors are far from convinced about the robustness of the system.

The signs are that nobody really wants a bust-up. Greek opinion polls suggest three-quarters of Greeks want to remain in the euro. And the euro zone can hardly relish the prospect of a Greek default and exit so soon after it agreed to a second bail-out for the country in March. Klaus Regling, head of the euro zone's rescue fund, the European Financial Stability Facility, said the euro zone has lent Greece €108 billion ($139 billion) in the past two months alone.

At the very least, euro-zone countries will want to avoid a break-up before July 1st, when the more powerful permanent rescue fund, the European Stability Mechanism, comes into force. German sources said this could be used to recapitalise fragile Spanish banks as a means of preventing the spread of contagion. Intriguingly, last night Mr Juncker said that €1 billion that had been withheld from the latest tranche of bail-out money to Greece in recent days would, after all, be paid out. Greek politicians seem to have convinced themselves that the euro zone is bluffing about ejecting their country. But Germany and others are determined to disabuse them. The recent menaces seem designed to achieve two goals: to exert pressure on Greeks to support more mainstream parties in a likely second election, and to prepare markets for the likelihood of Greece's departure if radicals are returned.

For now, attention turns to tonight's much-awaited meeting in Berlin between the new French president, François Hollande, and Angela Merkel, the German chancellor. The discussion will focus on Mr Hollande's call for a greater emphasis on stimulating growth (see my columns, here and here). But against a sharpening tone, his precise demands remain unclear. German ministers are worried he will press for a big stimulus, as well as for the mutualisation of debt through Eurobonds—as endorsed by a committee of the European Parliament.

Despite much talk of growth, on substance Mr Hollande did not seem to get much support from the euro group; if anything, he may have to embark on austerity himself. Though Mr Juncker said Europe needs a thorough debate on growth, he read out a statement from ministers declaring that the current strategy for fiscal consolidation (ie, austerity) "remains appropriate". Ministers praised two other rescued countries, Ireland and Portugal, for remaining "on track" with their adjustment programmes. And they were particularly effusive towards the Netherlands, whose parliament adopted a belt-tightening budget even after the government had fallen.

There was no sign of expected proposals from the European Commission to extend deadlines for some countries to reach their deficit targets. Nor did there seem to be much support for an Italian idea of excluding from the calculation of deficit targets some spending on "investment".

One issue Mr Hollande and Mrs Merkel will have to discuss is who should replace Mr Juncker as head of the euro group. The frontrunner is Wolfgang Schäuble, the German finance minister. But Mr Hollande may have misgivings about having a prominent German take over the job. After his performance tonight, Mr Juncker seems to have killed off the idea, favoured by some, that he would be asked to stay on.

EU says no risk to the eurozone because of Ireland's crisis

bioduniginla

November 25th, 2010

Current Location:

berlin

http://www.allvoices.com/contributed-news/7442070-eu-says-no-risk-to-the-eurozone-because-of-irelands-crisis

EU says no risk to the eurozone because of Ireland's crisis

BERLIN/PARIS | Thu Nov 25, 2010 10:56am EST

- Senior euro zone officials dismissed any risk of the single currency area breaking up after financial markets, alarmed by Ireland's debt crisis, forced the borrowing costs of Portugal and Spain to record highs.

"There is zero danger," Klaus Regling, chief of the euro's financial safety net, European Financial Stability Facility (EFSF), told German daily Bild in an interview published on Thursday when asked if the euro zone could break apart.

"It is inconceivable that the euro fails," he said.

Some economists and commentators, mostly in Britain and the United States, have suggested the 16-nation common currency launched in 1999 could split because of peripheral members' high debts and deficits, and a loss of competitiveness with Germany.

But Regling said: "No country will give up the euro of its own will: for weaker countries that would be economic suicide, likewise for the stronger countries. And politically Europe would only have half the value without the euro."

Greece received a three-year 110-billion-euro EU/IMF bailout in May, leading to the creation of the EFSF, which Ireland has now applied to tap to cope with the devastating impact of a banking crisis on its public finances.

The cost of insuring Irish debt against default continued to rise on Thursday amid market doubts about Dublin's austerity plan. In another sign of waning confidence, European clearing house LCH.Clearnet increased the deposit it requires traders in Irish government bonds to post for the third time this month.

The euro tumbled this week after German Chancellor Angela Merkel alarmed markets by saying the single currency was in an "exceptionally serious" situation.

German Bundesbank chief Axel Weber, a powerful member of the European Central Bank's governing council, said he was convinced EU leaders would do whatever it takes to repel what he called an "opportunistic attack" on the currency area.

Weber noted that the EFSF and other EU rescue funds had enough money, if necessary, to cover the borrowing needs of the four financially troubled members of the euro zone -- Greece, Ireland, Portugal and Spain.

"If that is not enough, I am convinced euro zone states will do what is necessary to protect the euro," Weber told French business and political leaders in Paris on Wednesday evening. "But 750 billion (euros) should be more than enough to see off an attack on the euro zone."

Currency and credit markets have been unnerved by German proposals to force bond holders to share the cost of any future default by highly indebted euro zone countries, as well as by the alarmist tone of recent comments by Merkel and European Council President Herman Van Rompuy.

ECB policymaker Ewald Nowotny voiced irritation at Merkel for not "differentiating between the euro as a currency and the problems of individual (euro zone) states."

Euro zone policymakers are hoping that Spain and Portugal can stave off an Irish- or Greek-style debt meltdown.

A Reuters poll this week showed 34 out of 50 analysts surveyed believe Portugal will be forced to follow Ireland and ask for help. In a separate survey only four out of 50 economists thought Spain would seek external aid.

The news from Europe is scarcely getting better. Germany and the rest of the EU are locked in a battle about how to introduce a banking union and mechanisms not only to end 'too big to fail' but also to provide funds for future bailouts, if necessary. Indeed, in an about face, we have moved from relying on bailouts to deal with financial crises to bail-ins. The recent Cyprus episode has contributed to further damaging everyone's reputation, including the IMF, a partner in the process, and revealed the EU's continued inability to offer credible and consistent policies.

Tensions over whether to soften existing austerity measures also persist. While Germany's finance minister has softened his stance on the issue, other German personalities, notably on the ECB's Executive Board, still maintain that fiscal consolidation remains essential. Any other policy is simply tantamount to following the 'road to perdition'. As if this is not enough, the U.K.'s government is preparing a referendum on EU membership and negotiating an exit from the EU.

Such battles might reflect the normal tensions that are to be expected, particularly when managing complex and incomplete arrangements that the EU and the euro zone represent, but they fail to capture the deep erosion of the European ideal that past generations of policy makers and politicians tried so hard to implement and popularize.

The following charts, from the PEW Research Centre, highlight the growing disenchantment with the European concept. Adding insult to injury the poll also reveals a growing gap between Germany, and the (mainly southern) periphery. Talk of a northern and a southern euro zone no longer seems as far-fetched as it was a year ago. More tellingly, one wonders whether the EU can survive the public turning its back on Europe as an entity.

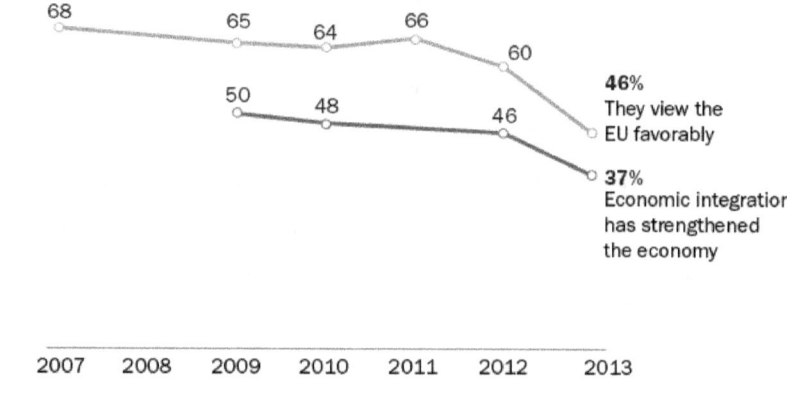

Median percent of European Union countries who say...

68   65   64   66

60

46%
They view the
EU favorably

50   48   46

37%
Economic integration
has strengthened
the economy

2007   2008   2009   2010   2011   2012   2013

Note: Median percentages for Britain, France, Germany, Spain, and Poland.
PEW RESEARCH CENTER

The drop in support for BOTH the EU and the concept of economic integration that is the cornerstone of the Maastricht Treaty has declined markedly. Only a relatively small minority sees the economic benefits of a single European market.

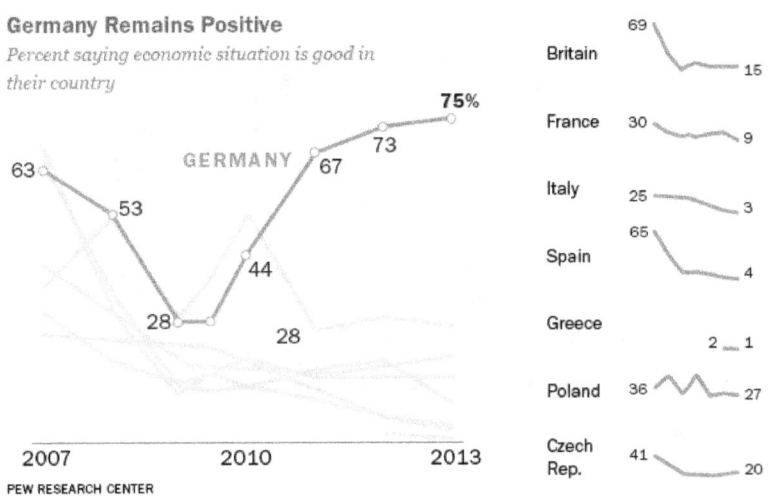

Germany Remains Positive

Percent saying economic situation is good in their country

GERMANY

75%

73

67

63

53

44

28

28

2007   2010   2013

PEW RESEARCH CENTER

Britain   69 — 15

France   30 — 9

Italy   25 — 3

Spain   65 — 4

Greece   2 _ 1

Poland   36 — 27

Czech Rep.   41 — 20

The above chart underscores the fact that Germany is increasingly alone in thinking that the overall economic situation is favorable. The drop in the economic 'mood' in large parts of Europe, is nothing short of spectacular. Indeed, the large number of single digits that represent the fraction of those polled who think the economic environment is 'good' is depressing.

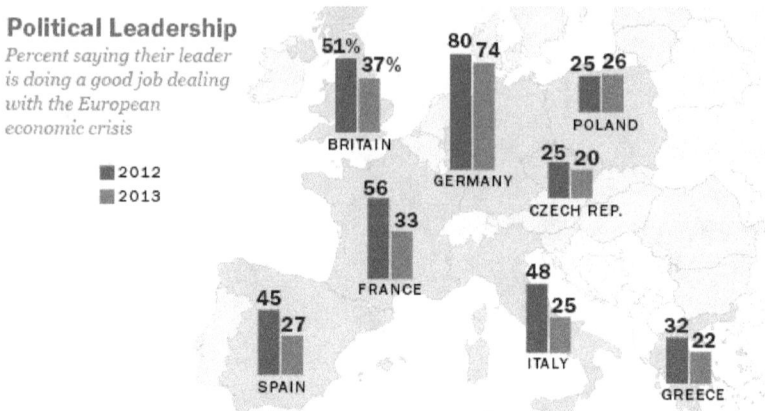

Political Leadership

Percent saying their leader is doing a good job dealing with the European economic crisis

■ 2012
■ 2013

BRITAIN 51% 37%

GERMANY 80 74

POLAND 25 26

CZECH REP. 25 20

FRANCE 56 33

SPAIN 45 27

ITALY 48 25

GREECE 32 22

Note: Asked about Chancellor Angela Merkel in Germany; Prime Minister David Cameron in Britian; Prime Minister Mariano Rajoy in Spain; Mario Monti in Italy; Prime Minister Donald Tusk in Poland; Prime Minister Petr Nečas in the Czech Republic; Prime Minister Antonis Samaras in Greece in 2013, Prime Minister Lucas Papademos in 2012; President Francois Hollande in France in 2013, President Nicolas Sarkozy in 2012.

PEW RESEARCH CENTER

A weak economy is not the only worry in Europe. Political leadership has taken a heavy beating almost everywhere. If there is poor leadership then where will the credible policies that will return the EU and the euro zone to growth come from?

IT'S been a week since shares in Bankia plummeted on reports, later denied, that customers were pulling deposits out of the Spanish lender. Fears of a full-scale bank run in Greece have not yet materialised. But the possibility of a deposit run in Europe's peripheral states is still very much alive. It is also the thing that policymakers are least prepared for.

As with most aspects to the euro crisis, the usual answers are not much help. One tactic is to show customers the money. Old hands of emerging-market bank runs talk of how they used to pile cash up in full view of panicking customers so that they could see how well stocked the banks were with money. The equivalent now is to let the central bank provide enough liquidity that the ATMs always spit out cash. But if the idea is to get your hands on euros today in case of a currency redenomination tomorrow, then you will still want it out of the bank and under the mattress.

Another response to runs is to calm worries about the solvency of specific institutions by beefing up the scale of deposit guarantees. In the first phase of the crisis, which now seems almost innocent in its simplicity, that is what governments did. But that makes the problem worse, not better, if government solvency is at the root of the problem.

The logical solution, as we argue this week, is to set up a joint deposit-guarantee scheme, in which euro-zone states pool resources to provide credible reassurance that depositors across the zone will get their money back, up to a harmonised threshold of €100,000 ($125,000). To get around the redenomination risk, the guarantee would have to be a promise to repay the original value of the deposit in euros.

The problem, as analysts have noted this week, is that even if the political will to realise this end existed (which is highly questionable), it would take a long time to negotiate an agreement. There are all sorts of fiddly details for Eurocrats to get their teeth into. Should the scheme be prefunded? Should depositors be preferred creditors, or behind the ECB in the queue? What supervisory arrangements are needed to ensure that creditor nations have sufficient oversight of the deposit-taking institutions they now insure in peripheral countries? And that is before you get into the rigmarole of ratifying agreements.

The trouble with this is that there is a horrible, insoluble mismatch between the timescales to which Europe's policymakers work and the timescale of a bank run. A run is most likely within the next few weeks. And if a run starts, Europe's governments will have to reassure within a matter of hours. You might just about get a communiqué from Brussels in that timeframe, but could it really reassure when so many questions are unanswered?

If it does not, then the run will continue until such time as the banks close their doors to further withdrawals or the central banks have satisfied depositors' demand for cash. The former means trapping depositors inside a system they do not trust. The latter means providing liquidity to a banking system that has been abandoned by its own citizens. It would be hard to come back from either position.

Eurozone facing 'survival crisis'

⛉ bioduniginla
November 16th, 2010
Current Location:
brussels

Brussels : Belgium | Nov 16, 2010 BY BiodunIginla 10

VIEWS: 0

Add your media to this report: Images | Videos Cell phones use report code: @7349726

EDIT REPORT

Tuesday, 16 November 2010

Topic: eurozone, ireland, bbc news

16 November 2010 Last updated at 06:38 ET Share this page

Facebook

Twitter

Share

Email

Print

by Natalie de Vallieres, BBC EU Desk, for the BBC's Biodun Iginla

Fears have grown that pressure will spread to other weaker eurozone countries Continue reading the main story Global Economy

Irish reluctant to take EU handout

Q&A: Irish bond crisis

Irish struggle with austerity

Currency war's key battlegrounds

The European Union is in a "survival crisis" over eurozone debt problems, the EU Council president has warned.Speaking hours before eurozone ministers meet to address threats to the bloc's economic stability, Herman Van Rompuy said that if the euro failed, so too would the EU.Members such as the Republic of Ireland and Portugal are under fresh scrutiny.Questions have been raised over whether they can manage their debt without help from EU funds.Mr Van Rompuy said he was "very confident" the problems could be overcome.But he added: "We all have to work together in order to survive with the eurozone, because if we don't survive with the eurozone we will not survive with the European Union." Bond auction Continue reading the main story "Start Quote When Ireland explicitly guaranteed the Irish banking system just over two years ago, the finance minister, Brian Lenihan, said it was 'the cheapest bank bailout in the world'. It is turning out to be very expensive" End Quote

Stephanie Flanders Economics editor, BBC News

Stephanomics: Crunch time

The Irish Republic has insisted it does not need EU help.But there is intense speculation that both it and Portugal may be forced to use EU bail-out money.Portugal's finance minister has said that investors believed that his country would be forced to seek emergency help, because of the worries spreading in the markets.Fernando Teixeira dos Santos urged Dublin to do the right thing for the euro and accept a bail-out.And the Spanish treasury secretary called on the Republic to act quickly to end market uncertainties.On Tuesday, Spain held an auction of government bonds - a routine way for governments to raise funds.However as Irish bail-out concerns hit other eurozone periphery countries, the rates it must pay on money borrowed - the bond yield - was higher than that faced earlier in the year. Solidarity sought The BBC's business editor Robert Peston said that much hinged on the stance of the European Central Bank (ECB) - which has propped up the Irish Republic's banking system with loans it could not get on the money markets

.Continue reading the main story div#ss-irish_econ {float:right;margin-left:10px;} div#ss-irish_econ h2.dslideshow-header {margin:0;padding:2px 0} div#ss-irish_econ dl.dslideshow-entry img {margin:0;} What went wrong in the Irish Republic The 1990s were good for the Irish Republic's economy, with low unemployment, high economic growth and strong exports creating the Celtic Tiger economy. Lots of multi-national companies set up in the Republic to take advantage of low tax rates. BACK 1 of 5 NEXT "Without the financial support of the ECB, Ireland would be bust right now," he said."But if there is the faintest sign that the ECB wants to withdraw the succour it has provided to weak eurozone banks, Ireland will no longer have a choice, it will have to go cap in hand either to its EU partners or to the IMF."

The Irish Republic's Europe Minister, Dick Roche, admitted that there were major liquidity problems at the country's banks.However, he said that his government had made major spending cuts which would be continued in its upcoming budget, and added that he hoped there would be "solidarity" from European colleagues at the Brussels meeting."I would hope after the meeting there would be more logic introduced into this," he told the BBC."There is no reason why we should trigger an IMF or an EU-type bail-out. There is a problem with liquidity in banks, there is no doubt about that. But I don't think that the appropriate response to that would be for the European finance ministers to panic."Continue reading the main story "Start Quote Dublin desperately wants to keep as much control of its own affairs as possible" End Quote

Mark Simpson BBC Ireland Correspondent

Irish reluctant to take EU handout

There are a range of funds which troubled nations could access - including the European Financial stability facility - 440bn-euro (£372bn) pot of money set up to aid eurozone countries that run into debt difficulties.And while the UK is not part of the eurozone, its taxpayers could end up footing some of the bill for any bail-outs.For example, there is the European Financial Stability Mechanism - a 60bn-euro, EU-wide scheme, which countries can draw on and to which the UK contributes 12%.Also, if the International Monetary Fund (IMF) is asked to step in, the UK would fund 4.5% of any aid. Budget brought forward? Continue reading the main story "Start Quote There would be a serious risk of a new credit crunch, and global recession, if the providers of that $1.5 trillion of credit to Ireland, Portugal and Greece were to lose confidence... and were to ask for their money back now" End Quote

Robert Peston Business editor, BBC News

Read Robert's blog

The Republic of Ireland government has consistently stated its determination to restore stability to the public finances and stressed that it is "fully funded" until late 2011.The banks have struggled since 2008, when the Irish Republic suffered a dramatic collapse of its property market.House values have fallen between 50% and 60% and bad debts - mainly in the form of loans to developers - have built up in the country's main banks, bringing them to the verge of collapse.Reports suggest the Republic will try to reassure markets by bringing forward details of its four-year financial plan to next week.The proposals will be severe. It has said it will impose unprecedented spending cuts or tax rises totalling 6bn euros (£5bn) to try to bring its underlying budget deficit down from about 12% to between 9.5 and 9.75% next year.While intended to boost confidence in the country's finances, investors fear the budget cuts could plunge the Republic back into recession, leading to further losses to the government via falling tax revenues and higher benefit payments. More on This Story Global Economy Background and Analysis

Irish reluctant to take EU handout

Q&A: Irish bond crisis

Irish struggle with austerity

Currency war's key battlegrounds

Latest News

Greece's budget deficit worsens

G20 agrees to address currencies

Recovery rates slow across Europe

Essentials

In graphics: Eurozone in crisis Compare unemployment levels, debt and deficits

Currency wars; what are they? Watch

Are US QE moves storing up trouble?

Q&A: What's moving the yen?

The euro-- The flight from Spain

♟ bioduniginla

July 27th, 2012

Current Location:

london, uk

by Natalie de Vallieres, Judith Stein, and Biodun Iginla, BBC News and The Economist

Spain can be shored up for a while; but its woes contain an alarming lesson for the entire euro zone

Jul 28th 2012 | from the print edition

-
-

THE worst nightmares are the ones you cannot wake up from. Just ask Spain. A year ago the cost of Spanish government borrowing soared as euro contagion spread from Greece, Ireland and Portugal. Panic seemed to subside with central-bank intervention and the promise of a new reforming government in Madrid. Since then Spain has, broadly, been as good as its word and Mariano Rajoy's government has cut budgets, freed its labour market, played its part in countless "make-or-break" summits in Brussels and secured up to €100 billion ($121 billion) to prop up its banks. Yet despite all its efforts and pain, Spain cannot shake off that sense of doom. On July 25th the yield on ten-year bonds touched a euro-era record of 7.75%. Two-year bonds have climbed above 7%: investors fear that Spain must soon ask for a bail-out—or default.

Spain's nightmare is a symptom of what is wrong with the entire euro zone. As the months drag on, the crisis is deepening. Europe's leaders have asked the world to trust that they will do what it takes to save the euro. They have also pleaded for more time to sort out the mess. Their task is indeed immense, but as they disappear to their chateaux and beach villas, trust is draining away and time is not their friend.

In this section

- Another fine mess
- »The flight from Spain
- Pray for the doves
- Colorado's dark night
- Aim for victory

Reprints

Related topics

- Financial markets
- World markets
- European markets
- Economies
- European economy

The bull and the horns

Spain's situation today is all the more shocking because only this month it had announced €65 billion of tax rises and spending cuts and won the funds for its bank rescue. This was meant to persuade investors that the whole euro zone is serious about keeping Spain. Yet the message was obliterated by news that the government now expects the recession to last into 2013 and, worse, that it will have to find the money to bail out regions which have suddenly confessed to being broke.

The prognosis for Spain is bleak (see article). The economy is in recession, the public sector is cutting spending and the private sector is reluctant to invest. This lack of domestic demand almost guarantees that Mr Rajoy will fail to meet the target to reduce the deficit. If that happens, Spain will be asked to impose yet more austerity. That will undermine his popularity, which has already fallen steeply since he was elected. Spain's resolve will be further damaged by rows over budget cuts between Madrid and regional politicians, who control 40% of public spending—and who, even if they are from Mr Rajoy's party, jealously guard their autonomy. Political uncertainty will feed back into the economy, which will only deteriorate more. And the vicious circle continues.

Spain cannot escape from this trap by itself. The government has admitted it does not have money to spare, and lenders are starting to doubt its solvency. A rescue of sorts can be cobbled together, with bond yields held down by some combination of the European Central Bank (ECB) and various rescue funds (even if the main one is still subject to a German constitutional court, whose judges are scandalously slow).

But that would only buy time. Perhaps not very much. Bail out Spain and immediately investors will rightly worry about Italy and whether the rescue funds are big enough. There are technical complications: new money from the rescue funds might count as senior debt, potentially leaving other creditors worse off. And political ones: the ECB cannot sustain huge intervention if Germany, its main shareholder, objects. Saving Spain will remain a short-term fix unless the euro zone genuinely unites around a plan that is economically sufficient and politically feasible.

Unite or die

Ultimately, as we have argued, a solution requires the currency's members to draw on their combined strength by mutualising some debt and standing behind their big banks. But alongside greater federalism, Europe also needs to do something about growth. Moderating austerity programmes is a priority (Spain shows how self-defeating they can be), but so is pursuing the structural reforms to set entrepreneurs free. Since 1975 the countries now in the euro zone have given birth to just one company currently among the world's 500 biggest (ironically it is from Spain: Inditex); by contrast California alone has created 26. Get rid of the mad rules that keep European business puny, and it could yet surprise everyone (see article).

That blueprint—greater federalism, a bail-out and pro-growth policies—would work, but it would take time. Even if the governments could today agree on what to do, haggling over the details, holding referendums and amending constitutions could easily take three years. The delay in even starting that process is only making a difficult task harder.

The trouble is that the 17 members of the euro zone, let alone their 333m citizens, cannot agree on who must sacrifice what to allow this new Europe to emerge. Germany, which this week was warned of a possible debt downgrade, is fearful that it is already being asked to pay too much. The Dutch and the Finns are also getting cross. France differs from Germany on what changes are needed in the way the EU is run (see Charlemagne). As for the debtors, in Greece voters are drifting from the centre to the political extremes. In Italy Mario Monti is the best prime minister in decades, but he is unelected, increasingly unpopular, and ever less able to see through the reforms his country needs. Instead, Silvio Berlusconi is contemplating a comeback—and he is outshone by an (intentional) comedian, who commands a fifth of the vote in polls.

The euro zone is stagnating (and dragging Britain down with it—see article). The crisis is engendering a combination of public-sector austerity and private-sector uncertainty. Investors hold back because they perceive some risk of a huge loss. Consumers save for the next rainy day. For as long as the catastrophic collapse of the euro zone remains a real possibility, it is hard to see that changing.

Perhaps the politicians will be shocked into action, by a euro-zone bank run, a chaotic Greek exit, or flight from Italian government debt. But Europe's leaders will find it increasingly hard to drag their people along with them. This is the deeper lesson of Spain's nightmare: delay is worsening the odds of the euro surviving.

IF SPAIN were a patient, the mood in the hospital ward would be tense. Every attempt by local specialists

advised by renowned European consultants to treat the sickness brings no more than temporary relief. Even more worrying, the relapses after each dose are happening sooner and sooner. Spain's chances of avoiding intensive care—a full bail-out—are receding to near vanishing-point.

The symptoms of Spanish sickness are manifest in ten-year government bond yields touching 7.75% on July 25th; previous bail-outs of Greece, Ireland and Portugal occurred not long after rates had surpassed 7%. Even more perturbing, two-year yields also briefly went above 7%, in effect foreclosing the government's ability to borrow at anything but short maturities.

In this section

- The Spanish patient
- Où est Monsieur Paulson?
- Unhappy birthday to you
- Taking stock
- The dismal dash
- Calories and currencies
- Downhill cycling
- The Chicago question

Reprints

Related topics

- Politics
- Spanish politics

- Italian politics
- German politics
- World politics

No isolation ward is possible in the financially integrated euro area and Spain's sickness quickly infected other countries. The Italian ten-year bond yield went above 6.5%, its highest since January. European stockmarkets retreated and Italy's fell to a euro-era low. Sentiment was further soured by a report from Moody's, a ratings agency, saying that Germany, Luxembourg and the Netherlands might lose their cherished triple-A status. The prognosis was based in part on fears about the public-debt burden that northern countries might have to assume if bail-outs spread.

The market funk was the more troubling since a Spanish government with a lot going for it had appeared to be getting a grip. Public

debt

is rising fast, but at 69% of GDP last year was far lower than Italy's 120%—and less even than Germany's 81%. The budget deficit is high (8.9% of GDP in 2011), but only a week before the market panic Mariano Rajoy, the prime minister, announced more tough austerity measures. And on July 20th European finance

ministers sanctioned the first tranche of a partial bail-out worth up to €100 billion ($121 billion) for Spanish banks.

So why are investors in such a cold sweat about Spain? One reason is that Mr Rajoy flunked hard choices at the outset, notably the cleansing of the banks. Despite a low starting-point for public

debt

, deficit overshoots have revealed insufficient central control over the 17 regions that are responsible for a big chunk of spending. Investors fret that more regions may follow Valencia, which applied for aid on July 20th. They are in any case sceptical that Spain can meet its targets for cutting the deficit in the teeth of a recession that is harsher than expected.

The biggest worry is Spain's external debt. Spain ran hefty current-account deficits in the first decade of the euro. As a result, its liabilities to foreign investors exceeded the assets that its residents own abroad by 92% of GDP last year, among the highest in the euro area. The problem for Spain is that foreign capital has been fleeing over the past year. That has weakened the banks and the economy and left the Spanish government shunned by foreign investors for its own financing needs.

The European summit in late June offered a flicker of hope but it is guttering. Euro-area leaders agreed that the European Stability Mechanism (ESM), their new permanent rescue fund, would be able to inject funds directly into banks rather than via loans to the government. That perked markets up since it promised to sever the link between weak banks and weak sovereigns. But before long the deal

looked less solid: the ESM cannot come into force until September, when Germany's constitutional court will rule on its legality. Assuming it passes that test, the ESM cannot be used for direct bank recapitalisation until a European supervisor is put in charge.

Spain may yet be able to fend off a bail-out for some time. It has some cash reserves and can still borrow at short maturities. The euro area also has its temporary rescue fund, which will lend the Spanish government the initial sum of money for the banks. But even if Spain survives a hot summer, the markets are signalling that it will need a full bail-out later this year.

That would be a nightmare, and not just for Spain. The Spanish government must borrow €385 billion until the end of 2014 to cover its budget deficit and other needs such as bond redemptions, according to economists at

Credit

Suisse. Even if the IMF chips in a third as in previous bail-outs, European lenders would have to find €250 billion or so. They have already committed €100 billion to rescuing Spanish banks, so for other emergencies they would have only €150 billion of the €500 billion now in their rescue kitties.

The course of events is eerily similar to what happened a year ago. Then European leaders appeared to have secured their summer holidays with a "breakthrough" summit. But things soon fell apart. Nerves about Italy and Spain were calmed only when the European Central Bank (ECB) started buying their bonds. The central bank was never keen on this and it has not been buying bonds for several months. Even if the ECB were to resume purchases they might be less effective than before, because its refusal to share in the pain of the Greek debt restructuring in March frightened bondholders elsewhere.

The awkward truth is that the Spanish government is not alone in flunking hard choices. The plight of Spain and the danger of its sickness spreading to Italy call for a decisive countermove by Germany and the ECB. One being discussed would be to give the ESM a banking licence, which would magnify its resources by allowing it to borrow from the central bank. The graver the euro crisis gets, the bigger the response has to be—and the harder it is to sell to sceptical northern electorates.

AS THE recession in the Eurozone moves into its sixth quarter and fiscal austerity continues, the importance of reviving credit supply to the private sector in order to stimulate output growth has become all the more apparent. In the European context boosting credit supply to the private sector requires a significant recovery in bank lending, given the relatively small size of the continent's corporate bond markets compared to those in the United States. In recent years although lending rates on commercial loans by European banks have not spiked in the same way as sovereign bond yields, the volume of lending has been very limited, see the evidence on this in European Central Bank surveys. Against a backdrop of tightening capital conditions and a poor growth outlook, any upturn in bank lending now depends critically on targeted interventions by the European Central Bank (ECB).

Despite a range of constraints on its ability to launch unconventional monetary policy measures, the ECB has played a key part in managing the Eurozone crisis, particularly through large scale and long maturity liquidity injections through its Long-Term RefinancingOperations. However, while not explicitly stated, the essential aim of such interventions has been to provide private banks with the funds necessary to stabilise sovereign debt markets in the Eurozone, in the absence of alternative adjustment mechanisms. The focus of the ECB must now turn to private lending and in particular a European version of the Bank of England's Funding for Lending Scheme, which ties central bank financing of commercial banks to increases in banks net lending in the real economy. Since its inception in 2012 the Bank of England scheme has supported a decline in lending spreads in the mortgage market (see this recent FT coverage). One reason to be optimistic about the prospects for some kind of economic recovery in Britain is that such a boost to the consumer sector combined with some delayed boost to exports through sterling depreciation will raise demand for business loans to exploit the potential supply of cheaper lending possible as a result of the Funding for Lending Scheme. A similar ECB initiative is necessary to address weaknesses in credit supply in the Eurozone. Without it, the prospects for lending growth and economic recovery are bleak, for the incentives to commit available bank funding to risky bank loans ahead of safe but less economically productive investments are very limited.

What are the prospects of ECB intervention of this kind? One implication of linking central bank funding to increases in commercial lending is that risk exposure for both private banks and central banks increases, and policy-makers at the ECB must be willing to demonstrate this kind of risk appetite. Hawkish policy-makers, particularly those linked to the Bundesbank, will no doubt cite risks to central bank capital and the potential inflation threat from action of this kind. On the other hand, the ECB has a longer history of accepting private securities and other risky instruments as collateral than do the Bank of England and the Federal Reserve (see for instance the review of the

ECB's recent monetary measures by Cour-Thimann and Winkler this recent issue of the Oxford Review of Economic Policy) and so linking its investments to private bank lending need not be interpreted as such a radical step. Furthermore, as the focus of such an initiative would be commercial banks rather than the governments of member states, the move is less likely to result in the legal disputes connected to existing unconventional ECB measures.

Ultimately, the ECB must overcome any obstacles to introducing a version of the Funding for Lending Scheme.

ANGELA MERKEL and François Hollande have broken the ice. Relations between the German chancellor and French president started frostily when Mr Hollande was elected last year, and became still chillier of late. They gave up the practice, common in the past, of cutting deals ahead of European summits. But now, as if to make up for lost time, they have drawn up a ten-page declaration in the run-up to the summit starting on June 27th.

Has the Franco-German motor restarted? To cynical Eurocrats, the partnership was always, in part, about hiding German strength and French weakness. With Germany unusually powerful and France unusually feeble, a long paper may provide the perfect cover. Pledges to fight youth unemployment are easy to make. But the tone of contempt for the European Commission will worry many smaller member states.

In this section

- Black sheep in the crimson dome

- Global ambitions v green concerns

- Princeling in trouble

- Devastating

- Winding down with a whimper

- **Crank up the motor**

Reprints

Related topics

- World markets

- European markets

- Financial markets

- Economics

- Economic integration

To many, the declaration is a German victory on substance and a French success on future form. Germany has delayed key moves in the creation of a banking union, especially an accord on the euro zone's rescue fund to recapitalise troubledbanks, until next year, well after the German general election.

In return, France won support for stronger "economic governance". There would be more summits of the 17 euro-zone leaders; a permanent president of the Eurogroup offinance ministers; and euro-zone-only meetings of other ministers, for example, of labour, industry and social affairs. This is all part of a peculiarly French obsession with creating a smaller, more exclusive and more overtly political Europe---to the exclusion of non-euro states such as Britain.

French and German officials claim to have made a breakthrough in setting up the pillars of a banking union by the middle of next year. The aim is to stop crippled banks and weak sovereigns from pulling each other down by creating European bodies to oversee the banks and deal with those that go bust. The issue boils down to two questions: Who decides? And who pays?

A euro-zone supervisor will begin work next year. But it is of limited use unless backed up by a European "resolution" body with the power to wind up or restructure crippled banks, ideally with access to common funds (see article). The trouble is, Germany does not want to pay for other countries' mess. Officials say this would violate the EU's treaties and, even if these could be bent, the German constitutional court would not wear it.

Thus a curious battle over terminology: the European Commission wanted a centralised resolution "authority"; leaders spoke of a "mechanism"; and Germany proposed a looser "network" of national resolution authorities and funds (yet to be created). The compromise drafted by Mrs Merkel and Mr Hollande speaks of a "board" involving national authorities. The declaration's next paragraph speaks of "an appropriate and effective private backstop arrangement". Here "arrangement" is in the singular, not in the plural, as in past EU documents.

Voilà! claim the French. With a single letter the Germans have crossed the Rubicon. They accept that they can be overruled by a European authority that can use pooled money (raised from the banks themselves). Not quite, reply the Germans. For a decade or more, the resolution fund will be short of money. Any bank wind-up will thus rely on the taxpayer. And the use of German cash will require a vote in the German parliament. Expect months of wrangling after the commission issues its formal proposal later this month.

And what of "economic governance"? Fiscal rules have been toughened in the crisis. The commission is charged with monitoring budgets and "economic imbalances". There are binding sanctions for rule-breakers, and the commission can recommend detailed reforms. As the recession has deepened, the emphasis has shifted from deficit-cutting to promoting structural reforms. But the commission is operating at the limit of its legal powers and of political acceptance. A plan to have countries sign "contracts" to enact reforms, perhaps in exchange for money, is stuck.

The commission's diktat

Last month France was delighted to be granted two more years to meet its deficit target of 3% of GDP. Yet Mr Hollande bridled when the commission urged him to overhaul pensions and cut spending as well as liberalise the economy. "The commission cannot dictate to us what we should do," he declared.

For the French, economic policy cannot be left to unknown technocrats in Brussels. Democratic legitimacy requires that its broad outline be debated and agreed by *les chefs*. Would pension reform be any more palatable if dictated by Mrs Merkel rather than by commissioners? Surely not. But among his peers, a French president is better able to block reforms he dislikes, or at least to trade them for concessions, such as harmonising taxes and adopting a minimum wage across the euro zone.

Most European countries dislike Franco-German stitch-ups, but are even more upset when the two cannot agree. If the euro zone is ever to be pulled out of the mire, the Franco-German motor must work. A compromise between France and Germany, because they are so different, usually wins the support of others. But not all agreements are equally desirable.

A good deal would see Germany agree to an effective banking union that pools at least some of the risks in the euro zone, while France accepts the need to liberalise its economy, deepen Europe's single market and drop barriers to international trade. The danger is that Mrs Merkel and Mr Hollande will strike a bad deal: create a half-baked banking union that fails to stabilise the euro zone, allows France to avoid necessary reforms and blunts the competitiveness of everybody else. That might be worse than no agreement at all.

Understanding Europe

After the darkest hour

How post-war peace turned into the euro crisis

May 25th 2013 |From the print edition

-
-

The Passage to Europe: How a Continent Became a Union. By Luuk van Middelaar. Translated by Liz Waters. *Yale University Press; 352 pages: $40 and £25*. Buy from Amazon.com, Amazon.co.uk

The Lost Continent. By Gavin Hewitt. *Hodder & Stoughton; 368 pages; £20*. Buy from Amazon.co.uk

In this section

- Beyond the numbers
- Infernal triangle
- What a Burke
- A bug's life
- After the darkest hour
- Eye music

Reprints

Related topics

- Europe
- Amazon
- German politics
- European politics
- World politics

THE euro crisis grinds on. But, because markets no longer fear the single currency's immediate break-up, it has faded from the headlines. So this is a sensible moment to debate the direction of the European Union. And a good place to start is by analysing the political dynamic that shaped today's EU—something that is very well done in Luuk van Middelaar's book, which deservedly won the European book prize in 2012 and is now published for the first time in English.

Mr Van Middelaar is a Dutch political philosopher who works for Herman Van Rompuy, president of the European Council. His thesis is that the EU is best understood as three concentric spheres. The inner one contains the Brussels institutions; the outer one non-EU Europe. But it is the middle one that is the most interesting and most crucial: member countries and their governments. In his model the EU is not a federal union like America. It is a loose confederation, in which national governments are the main sources of power.

The author describes the politics of the European project that produced this model with historical accuracy and some verve. For an Anglo-Saxon readership, his material on the early years is particularly valuable: how in the early 1960s the European Court of Justice established the supremacy of European law; the story of de Gaulle, the veto and the so-called Luxembourg compromise; and, in the early 1970s, the arrival of the European Council of heads of government with, as a quid pro quo, direct elections to the European Parliament.

This system produces many tensions. As the euro saga has shown, the driver of EU policy is the European Council. It is this body (often in its smaller euro-zone formation) that decides on bail-outs, banking union and so on deep into the Brussels night. But it is Germany's Angela Merkel, not Mr Van Rompuy or the European Commission's president, José Manuel Barroso, who is Europe's most powerful leader.

Yet as more power over economic policy is transferred to European level because of the euro crisis, legitimacy is being eroded. The commission, which enforces the rules, is unelected and has lost influence. The author is not a fan of the European Parliament as a vehicle for democratic input. It acts more like a pressure group lobbying for increases in its own powers. He hankers for a bigger role for national parliaments, but it is hard to see how this might emerge from today's institutional set-up.

Intriguingly, most of Mr Van Middelaar's book was written before the euro crisis; he adds a prologue to the new English version. Yet his account fits the crisis well, and it has much to teach those who want to understand the EU's recent political dynamic.

Those who prefer a blow-by-blow account of the horrors of the euro drama can turn instead to Gavin Hewitt's "The Lost Continent". The BBC's Europe editor tells the tale of what he calls Europe's darkest hour since the war. He makes no pretence at deep analysis or intellectual theorising. But he covers the main moments, both tragic and comic, and the nature of its protagonists, from George Papandreou in Greece to Brian Cowan in Ireland and Silvio Berlusconi in Italy.

How will it all finish? Neither author says. But it is difficult to be confident that Mr Hewitt's darkest hour will quickly be transformed into light. And the tensions in Mr Van Middelaar's model could easily stretch the entire system to breaking-point. The critical test will be whether, after three years of austerity and 18 months of recession, Europe finds a way to reinvigorate economic growth. Without that, a happy ending seems unlikely.

The euro-zone economy

Recession, cont'd

Shrinking output may prompt the European Central Bank to ease further

May 18th 2013 |From the print edition

-
-

ONE euro crisis may be over, but another has begun. The single currency is no longer under siege in financial markets, but it will not prove politically viable unless growth returns. Any residual hopes of an early recovery were dashed by GDP figures published on May 15th. These showed the euro zone still mired in recession.

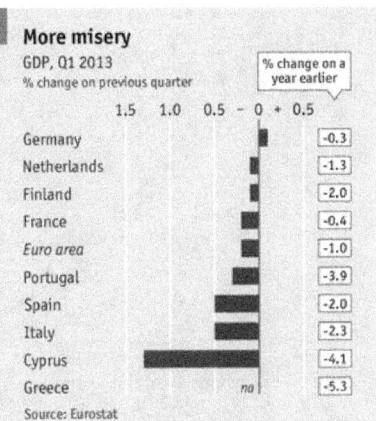

More misery
GDP, Q1 2013
% change on previous quarter

	% change on a year earlier
Germany	-0.3
Netherlands	-1.3
Finland	-2.0
France	-0.4
Euro area	-1.0
Portugal	-3.9
Spain	-2.0
Italy	-2.3
Cyprus	-4.1
Greece	-5.3

Source: Eurostat

Euro-area output shrank in the first three months of this year by 0.2% compared with its level in the final quarter of 2012 (see chart). That decline, which was a bit worse than expected, left GDP 1%

lower than a year ago. Output has now contracted for six consecutive quarters in a recession stretching back to late 2011.

In this section

- Libor in a barrel
- Boom and gloom
- Too much information
- Caveat voter
- The lure of the Bosphorus
- Recession, cont'd
- Don't worry, be happy
- The humble hero

Reprints

Related topics

- Spain
- Germany
- Recessions and depressions
- European Central Bank
- World markets

The downturn is still steepest in southern Europe. Output fell by 0.5% in both Italy and Spain, the third- and fourth-biggest economies in the euro zone. But GDP is now declining in most euro-zone countries, including France, the area's second-largest economy, which is back in recession following a second quarter of declining output, of 0.2%. The main exception remains Germany, the biggest economy, though it barely grew in the first three months of this year. Output was up by a lower-than-expected 0.1% (following a 0.7% fall in late 2012).

The recession could well drag on for yet another quarter. Based on a recent survey of purchasing managers, output in services and manufacturing continued to shrink last month. Even if a recovery does get under way later this year, it will probably be a feeble affair. Earlier this month the European Commission forecast that annual GDP would fall by 0.4% this year and that it would grow by only 1.2% in 2014.

The danger is that even if growth does reappear it will be detectable only in decimal-point statistics and not in people's lives. The biggest risk stems from unemployment, which now stands at 12.1% in the euro area, the highest on records going back to 1995. That overall rate masks a sharp contrast between Germany, where it is just 5.4%, and Spain and Greece, where it has reached 27%. The disparity is still greater for youth unemployment, which ranges from 7.6% in Germany to 56% in Spain and 64% in Greece.

Earlier this month the European Central Bank (ECB) brought down its main policy rate, from 0.75% to 0.5%. This week's poor GDP figures will increase pressure on the ECB to take further action to foster a recovery when its governing council meets in early June.

FOR the past three years America's leaders have looked on Europe's management of the euro crisis with barely disguised contempt. In the White House and on Capitol Hill there has been incredulity that Europe's politicians could be so incompetent at handling an economic problem; so addicted to last-minute, short-term fixes; and so incapable of agreeing on a long-term strategy for the single currency.

Those criticisms were all valid, but now those who made them should take the planks from their own eyes. America's economy may not be in as bad a state as Europe's, but the failures of its politicians—epitomised by this week's 11th-hour deal to avoid the calamity of the "fiscal cliff"—suggest that Washington's pattern of dysfunction is disturbingly similar to the euro zone's in three depressing ways.

In this section

- »America's European moment
- Down-turn Abe
- Rape and murder in Delhi
- Dawn in the west
- Divided they fall

Reprints

Can-kicking is a transatlantic sport

The first is an inability to get beyond patching up. The euro crisis deepened because Europe's politicians serially failed to solve the single currency's structural weaknesses, resorting instead to a succession of temporary fixes, usually negotiated well after midnight. America's problems are different. Rather than facing an imminent debt crisis, as many European countries do, it needs to deal with the huge long-term gap between tax revenue and spending promises, particularly on health care, while not squeezing the economy too much in the short term. But its politicians now show themselves similarly addicted to kicking the can down the road at the last minute.

This week's agreement, hammered out between Republican senators and the White House on New Year's Eve, passed by the Senate in the early hours of New Year's Day and by the House of Representatives later the same day, averted the spectre of recession. It eliminated most of the sweeping tax increases that were otherwise due to take effect from January 1st, except for those on the very wealthy, and temporarily put off all the threatened spending cuts (see article). Like many of Europe's crisis summits, that staved off complete disaster: rather than squeezing 5% out of the economy (as the fiscal cliff implied) there will now be a more manageable fiscal squeeze of just over 1% of GDP in 2013. Markets rallied in relief.

But for how long? The automatic spending cuts have merely been postponed for two months, by which time Congress must also vote to increase the country's debt ceiling if the Treasury is to be able to go on paying its bills. So more budgetary brinkmanship will be on display in the coming weeks.

And the temporary fix ignored America's underlying fiscal problems. It did nothing to control the unsustainable path of "entitlement" spending on pensions and health care (the latter is on track to double as a share of GDP over the next 25 years); nothing to rationalise America's hideously complex and distorting tax code, which includes more than $1 trillion of deductions; and virtually nothing to close America's big structural budget deficit. (Putting up tax rates at the very top simply does not raise much money.) Viewed through anything other than a two-month prism, it was an abject failure. The final deal raised less tax revenue than John Boehner, the Republican speaker in the House of Representatives, once offered during the negotiations, and it included none of the entitlement reforms that President Barack Obama was once prepared to contemplate.

The reason behind this lamentable outcome is the outsize influence of narrow interest groups—which marks a second, unhappy parallel with Europe. The inability of Europeans to rise above petty national concerns, whether over who pays for bail-outs or who controls bank supervision, has prevented them from making the big compromises necessary to secure the single currency's future. America's Democrats and Republicans have proved similarly incapable of reaching a grand bargain;

both are far too driven by their parties' extremists and too focused on winning concessions from the other side to work steadily together to secure the country's fiscal future.

The third parallel is that politicians have failed to be honest with voters. Just as Chancellor Angela Merkel and President François Hollande have avoided coming clean to the Germans and the French about what it will take to save the single currency, so neither Mr Obama nor the Republican leaders have been brave enough to tell Americans what it will really take to fix the fiscal mess. Democrats pretend that no changes are necessary to Medicare (health care for the elderly) or Social Security (pensions). Republican solutions always involve unspecified spending cuts, and they regard any tax rise as socialism. Each side prefers to denounce the other, reinforcing the very polarisation that is preventing progress.

Fixed today, hobbled tomorrow

Optimists will point out that America is unlikely to face a European-style debt crisis in the near future, but the slow-burning fuse is itself a problem. One positive side-effect of Europe's crisis is that it has forced euro-zone countries to raise their retirement ages and rationalise pensions and health-care promises. America, which has the biggest structural budget deficit in the rich world bar Japan, will become an outlier in its failure to deal with the fiscal consequences of an ageing population. Its ageing is slower than Europe's but, as its debt piles up and business and consumer confidence is dampened, the eventual crunch will be more painful.

The saddest thing about this week's deal is how unaware Messrs Obama and Boehner seem to be of the wider damage their petty partisanship is doing to their country. National security is not just about the number of tanks or rockets you have. As it has failed to deal with the single currency, Europe's standing has crumbled in the world. Why should developing countries trust American leadership, when it seems incapable of solving anything at home? And while the West's foremost democracy

stays paralysed, China is making decisions and forging ahead.

This week Mr Obama boasted that he had fulfilled his mandate by raising taxes on the rich. In fact,

by failing once again to clear up America's fundamental fiscal trouble, he and Republican leaders are

building Brussels on the Potomac.

Posted 5 months ago

#fiscal cliff #us economy #eurozone crisis #BBC News #The Economist #biodun iginla

0 notes

SO GRAVE, so menacing, so unstoppable has the euro crisis become that

even rescue talk only fuels ever-rising panic. Investors have sniffed

out that Europe's leaders seem unwilling ever to do enough. Yet unless

politicians act fast to persuade the world that their desire to preserve

the euro is greater than the markets' ability to bet against it, the

single currency faces ruin. As credit lines gum up and outsiders plead

for action, it is not just the euro that is at risk, but the future of

the European Union and the health of the world economy.

It is a sobering thought that so much depends on the leadership of

squabbling European politicians who still consistently underestimate what confronts them (see article).

But the only way to stop the downward spiral now is an act of supreme

collective will by euro-zone governments to erect a barrage of financial

measures to stave off the crisis and put the governance of the euro on a

sounder footing.

In this section

- »How to save the euro
- Justice
- delayed
- Good
- fences
- Out
- with the old

Reprints

Related topics
- Political policy
- Financial rescue plans
- Economic policy
- Domestic policy
- Germany

The costs will be large. Few people, least of all this newspaper,
want either vast intervention in financial markets or a big shift of

national sovereignty to Europe. Nor do many welcome a bigger divide

between the 17 countries of the euro zone and the EU's remaining ten. It

is just that the alternatives are far worse. That is the blunt truth

that Germany's Angela Merkel, in particular, urgently needs to explain to her people.

The failure of austerity and pretence

A rescue must do four things fast. First, it must make clear which of Europe's governments are deemed illiquid and which are insolvent, giving unlimited backing to the solvent governments but restructuring the debt of those that can never repay it. Second, it has to shore up Europe's banks to ensure they can withstand a sovereign default. Third, it needs to shift the euro zone's macroeconomic policy from its obsession with budget-cutting towards an agenda for growth. And finally, it must start the process of designing a new system to stop such a mess ever being created again.

The fourth part will take a long time to complete: it will involve new treaties and approval by parliaments and voters. The others need to be decided on speedily (say over a weekend, when the markets are shut) with the clear aim that European governments and the European Central Bank (ECB) act together to end today's vicious circle of panic, in which the weakness of government finances, the fragility of banks and worries about low growth all feed on each other.

So far the euro zone's response has relied too much on two things: austerity and pretence. Sharply cutting budget deficits has been the priority—hence the tax rises and spending cuts. But this collectively huge fiscal contraction is self-defeating. By driving enfeebled economies into recession it only increases worries about both government debts and European banks (see article).

And mere budget-cutting does not deal with the real cause of the mess, which is a loss of credibility.

Italy and Spain are under attack not because their finances have suddenly deteriorated, but because investors fret that they may be forced to default. For this loss of confidence, blame the pretence. Europe's leaders have repeatedly denied that Greece is insolvent (when everyone knows it is), failing to draw a line between it and the likes of Spain and Italy, which are solvent but short of liquidity. The excuse is that a Greek restructuring may cause contagion. In fact denying the inevitable has undermined pledges about solvent governments.

Instead of austerity and pretence, a credible rescue should start with growth and, where it is unavoidable, a serious restructuring of debt. Europe must make an honest judgment about which side of the line countries are on. Greece, which is unambiguously insolvent, ought to have a hard but orderly write-down. The latest, inadequate plan for a second Greek bail-out, agreed at a summit in July, should be thrown away and rewritten. But all the other euro members (and on present numbers Portugal is just about in the solvent camp) should be defended with overwhelming financial firepower. All the troubled economies, solvent or insolvent, need a renewed programme of structural reform and liberalisation. Freeing up services and professions, privatising companies, cutting bureaucracy and delaying retirement will create conditions for renewed growth—and that is the best way to reduce debts.

How to prevent contagion? A Greek default would threaten many banks, not just in Greece: this week the markets took aim at French banks that hold southern European debt. Moreover, solvent countries need a breathing-space to push through reforms. That points to agreeing to two measures at the same time: a scheme to shore up the banks, which may take months to put into practice, and a rock-solid promise to support solvent governments, which has to be immediate.

The recapitalisation of Europe's banks must be based on proper stress tests (which should this time include possible default on Greek sovereign debts). Some banks may be able to raise money in the equity markets, but the most vulnerable will need government help. Core countries like Germany and the Netherlands have enough cash to look after their own banks, but peripheral governments may need euro-zone money. Ideally that would come from the European Financial Stability Facility (EFSF), whose overhaul was the most useful thing to emerge from the July summit. But it also makes sense to set up a euro-zone bank fund, together with a euro-zone bank-resolution authority. That is part of the longer-term institution building. However, the ECB could help the banks by giving a commitment to provide unlimited liquidity for as long as it is required, rather than a rolling six months, as now.

The great firewall of Europe

None of this will work unless the Europeans create a firewall around the solvent governments. That means shoring up euro-zone sovereign debt. Spain and Italy owe €2.5 trillion. What if the markets suddenly took fright over Belgium or France? Some have argued for a system of Eurobonds in which every country's debt is backed by all. But the political oversight to ensure that high-spending countries do not fritter away other people's money would take years to sort out—and one thing the euro zone does not have is time. The answer is to turn to the only institution that can credibly counter a collective loss of confidence on such a scale.

The ECB must declare that it stands behind all solvent countries' sovereign debts and that it is ready to use unlimited resources to ward off market panic. That is consistent with the ECB's goal to ensure price and financial stability for the euro zone as a whole. So long as governments are solvent and the bank sells the bonds back to the market after the crisis, this does not amount to monetising government debt. In today's recessionary world, the ECB could buy several trillion euros-worth of bonds without unleashing inflation.

Even so, this is a huge step. The ECB's German officials have taken

to resigning in protest at the limited bond-buying undertaken so far.

They fear not only that so young an institution is vulnerable to a loss

of credibility, but also that the ECB, which is independent but

unelected, could become embroiled in political decisions—especially by

declaring a state insolvent and cutting it off. Both these longer-term

risks are real, but they are far outweighed by the need to stop the rot.

It would be a nonsense if the ECB's dogged defence of monetary rigour

led, say, to an Italian default and a global depression.

A bad deal, or a much worse one?

Put our plan to many Europeans—creditor Germans, debtor Greeks or

Eurosceptic Britons—and they may moan that this is not what they were

promised when the euro was set up. Completely true, and sadly

irrelevant. The issue now is not whether the euro was mis-sold or

whether it was a terrible idea in the first place; it is whether it is

worth saving. Would it be cheaper to break it up now? And are the longer-term political costs of redesigning Europe to save the euro too great?

The sobering truth about the single currency is that getting in is a lot easier than getting out again. Legally, the euro has no exit clause. If Greece stormed out, and damn the law, as it might yet have to do, it would suffer a run on its banks, as depositors withdrew euros before they were forcibly converted into devalued new drachma. It would have to impose capital controls. Greek companies with international bills would risk bankruptcy, as they would suddenly be without the cash to cover them; and the pressure on other wobbly countries would increase. That is why we favour restructuring Greece, but letting it stay in the euro.

If, on the other hand, a strong country like Germany walked out of the euro, probably taking other strong countries with it, the result would be just as terrible. The new hard currency would soar, hitting German exporters. Turmoil in the rump of the euro zone would batter export markets just as the north's firms became less competitive. German banks and companies, in a mirror image of what would happen in Greece, would suffer from the sudden devaluation of euro assets outside the new hard-currency zone. And the rump might still break apart, as Italy or Spain would not want anything to do with Greece. Amid the debris of broken treaties, wild currency swings and bitter recriminations, Europe's single market could collapse and the EU itself—the rock of the continent's post-war stability—could start to crumble.

Attaching hard numbers to any of this is difficult. Analysts at UBS, a bank, reckon that euro break-up could cost a peripheral country 40-50% of GDP in the first year, and a core country 20-25% (see article). Yes, that is a guess (as are the various estimates for the ongoing costs of break-up and those of a bail-out in future years). But the immediate bill for a break-up of the single currency would surely be in the trillions of euros. By contrast, a successful rescue would seem a bargain. Add together the money already spent on rescues, to what is needed to recapitalise European banks and any potential losses to the ECB, and the total will still only be in the hundreds of billions of euros. If the ECB's intervention is bold and credible it might not even have to buy that much debt, because investors would step in. In short,

the euro zone would be reckless to flirt with collapse when an

affordable rescue is possible.

German taxpayers might accept that the immediate costs of our rescue

plan are smaller than break-up. But what they detest is the idea that it

might let feckless Italians and Portuguese off the hook. Safe in the

knowledge that the ECB stands behind their bonds, they may shy away from

reform and rectitude.

Two risks flow from this. The immediate (and real) one is that

furious Germans will demand that Greece is thrown out (or bullied out)

of the euro to frighten the others. Such a horrific event would indeed

scare Portugal and Ireland, but a threat to expel Italy or Spain is

empty: they are too big and too tightly tied into the EU. Simply

chucking out Greece because it was convenient would permanently

undermine the security of small members of the EU. Besides, once Greece

defaults and restructures, its economy stands a good chance of making a

credible start on its long journey to economic health.

The longer-term risk has to do with "more Europe". Fans of political integration say that the only way to enforce discipline is to create a United States of Europe (see Charlemagne). Perhaps a fiscal union that would supervise the issuance of common Eurobonds? Or a new supervisory role for euro-zone governments, or, heaven forbid, the useless European Parliament? Somewhere behind this also looms the idea that the ins will now be able to boss around the outs. The ten countries, including Sweden, Poland and Britain, that kept their own currencies may face a choice: to join the euro or be excluded from a new "core Europe", which in effect starts setting policies. And, this being Europe, there is every chance that the politicians will try to avoid discussing a lot of this with their electorates.

The Economist concedes that our rescue plan begins with a democratic deficit that needs to be fixed if steps towards closer fiscal union are to work. But there must be ways for good governments to force bad ones to keep in line that do not require the building of a huge new federal superstate. The Dutch have suggested a commissioner in Brussels with power to veto countries' fiscal excesses, and to impose his judgments by law. Mrs Merkel has talked of giving the European Court of Justice the right to impose good behaviour. These are big steps—make no mistake—and because they involve treaty changes they would have to be sold to voters. But they are a long way short of a United States of Europe.

Mrs Merkel, it's time to explain the choices

The outs, in particular, may still be nervous about all this. So frankly is this newspaper. But the alternative may be the collapse of not just the single currency but the single market and the whole European project. The euro has reached the point where nobody is going to get what they want—something that needs to be spelled out to the Germans more than anybody. Over the past 18 months they have grudgingly supported half-rescue after half-rescue—and the bill has gone up. In the end confidence and credibility are all. For the ECB to stand behind less prudent countries may be unwelcome to Germans; but letting the euro fall to bits is much, much worse. Spell that out clearly to your voters, Mrs Merkel.

Torn Apart at the Seams: Is Europe failing?

The news from Europe is scarcely getting better. Germany and the rest of the EU are locked in a battle about how to introduce a banking union and mechanisms not only to end 'too big to fail' but also to provide funds for future bailouts, if necessary. Indeed, in an about face, we have moved from relying on bailouts to deal with financial crises to bail-ins. The recent Cyprus episode has contributed to further damaging everyone's reputation, including the IMF, a partner in the process, and revealed the EU's continued inability to offer credible and consistent policies.

Tensions over whether to soften existing austerity measures also persist. While Germany's finance minister has softened his stance on the issue, other German personalities, notably on the ECB's Executive Board, still maintain that fiscal consolidation remains essential. Any other policy is simply tantamount to following the 'road to perdition'. As if this is not enough, the U.K.'s government is preparing a referendum on EU membership and negotiating an exit from the EU.

Such battles might reflect the normal tensions that are to be expected, particularly when managing complex and incomplete arrangements that the EU and the euro zone represent, but they fail to capture the deep erosion of the European ideal that past generations of policy makers and politicians tried so hard to implement and popularize.

The following charts, from the PEW Research Centre, highlight the growing disenchantment with the European concept. Adding insult to injury the poll also reveals a growing gap between Germany, and the (mainly southern) periphery. Talk of a northern and a southern euro zone no longer seems as far-fetched as it was a year ago. More tellingly, one wonders whether the EU can survive the public turning its back on Europe as an entity.

Median percent of European Union countries who say...

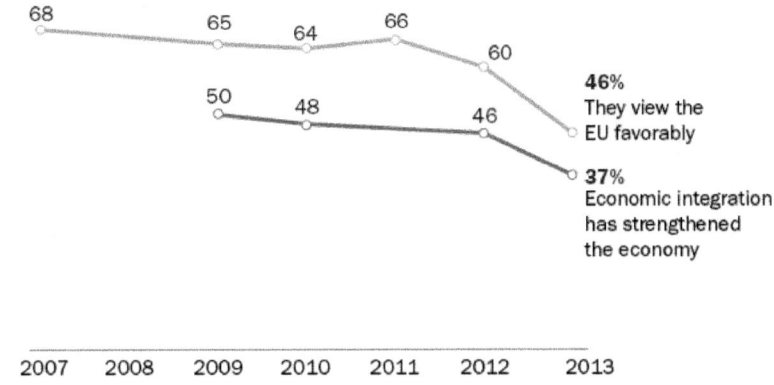

68
65
64
66
60

50
48
46

46%
They view the
EU favorably

37%
Economic integration
has strengthened
the economy

2007   2008   2009   2010   2011   2012   2013

Note: Median percentages for Britain, France, Germany, Spain, and Poland.
PEW RESEARCH CENTER

The drop in support for BOTH the EU and the concept of economic integration that is the cornerstone of the Maastricht Treaty has declined markedly. Only a relatively small minority sees the economic benefits of a single European market.

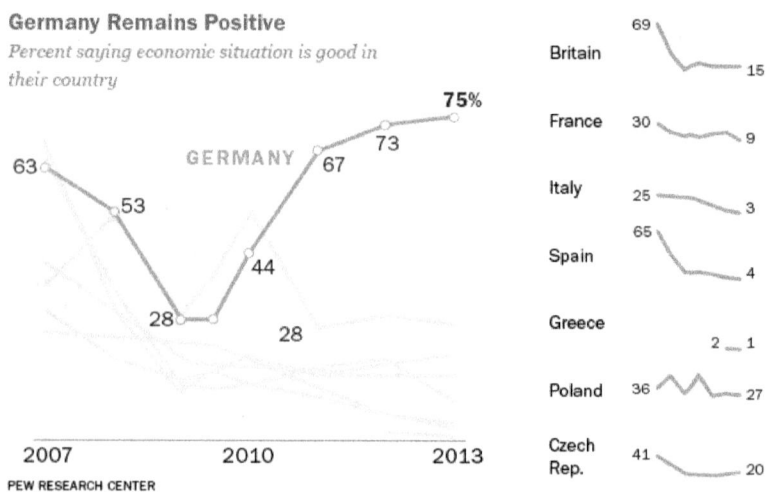

Germany Remains Positive

Percent saying economic situation is good in their country

GERMANY

63
53
28 — 28
44
67
73
75%

2007   2010   2013

PEW RESEARCH CENTER

Britain   69 ⌐ 15
France   30 ⌐ 9
Italy   25 — 3
Spain   65 ⌐ 4
Greece   2 — 1
Poland   36 ⌐ 27
Czech Rep.   41 ⌐ 20

The above chart underscores the fact that Germany is increasingly alone in thinking that the overall economic situation is favorable. The drop in the economic 'mood' in large parts of Europe, is nothing short of spectacular. Indeed, the large number of single digits that represent the fraction of those polled who think the economic environment is 'good' is depressing.

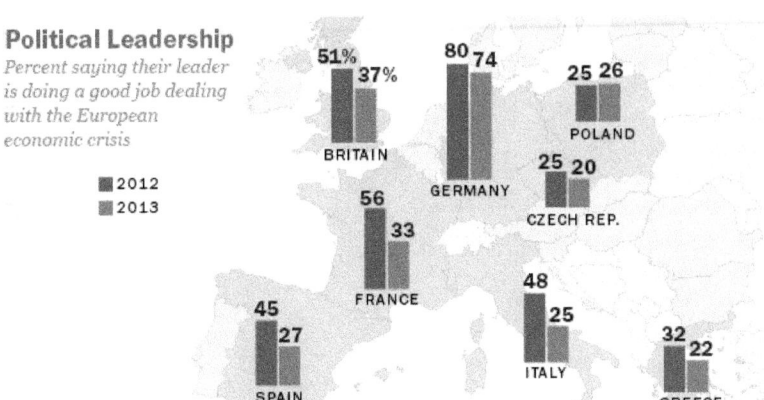

Political Leadership

Percent saying their leader is doing a good job dealing with the European economic crisis

- ■ 2012
- ■ 2013

BRITAIN 51% 37%

GERMANY 80 74

POLAND 25 26

CZECH REP. 25 20

FRANCE 56 33

SPAIN 45 27

ITALY 48 25

GREECE 32 22

Note: Asked about Chancellor Angela Merkel in Germany; Prime Minister David Cameron in Britian; Prime Minister Mariano Rajoy in Spain; Mario Monti in Italy; Prime Minister Donald Tusk in Poland; Prime Minister Petr Nečas in the Czech Republic; Prime Minister Antonis Samaras in Greece in 2013, Prime Minister Lucas Papademos in 2012; President Francois Hollande in France in 2013, President Nicolas Sarkozy in 2012.

A weak economy is not the only worry in Europe. Political leadership has taken a heavy beating almost everywhere. If there is poor leadership then where will the credible policies that will return the EU and the euro zone to growth come from?

The euro crisis

Less money, more problems

Jun 11th 2013, 13:57 by R.A. | WASHINGTON

- •
- •

EUROPE has lots of economic problems, of the sort that will tend to make a place poorer over time. But it has one very big problem, of the sort that can condemn an economy to prolonged recession. Mario Dragio laid it bare last week in comments following the European Central Bank's latest policy statement:

Question: You talked about dramatism a few minutes ago and I am afraid I will be a little bit dramatic now because I am from a country that has an unemployment rate of 27%, which is a number of a great depression, a fiscal policy that is contractionary and a monetary policy in Spain and also in other countries that is also contractionary because credit is not available to small and medium-sized companies. Are you telling the Spanish, Portuguese, Irish or even Italian people that the ECB can't do anything else with inflation actually lower than 2%?

Draghi: Well, I am not sure I get the point, but I think I get it. First, the fact that inflation is low is not, by itself, bad; with low inflation, you can buy more stuff.

This statement was rightly greeted by groans and forehead slaps around the macroeconomic world. It is particularly depressing, as Paul Krugman says, because Mr Draghi is a good economist and probably the best president the ECB could hope to have.

Why is this so problematic? As Mr Draghi surely knows, prices have microeconomic content and macroeconomic content. The price of a movie ticket or a gallon of petrol might go up or down in response to short-run supply and demand fundamentals: that's microeconomic content. Shifts in market activity become reflected in prices, triggering a response from firms and households to ensure that resources are used (more or less) optimally. And yes, if the price of petrol falls you can either buy more petrol or use the money saved on the fixed quantity of petrol you buy to purchase more of other things: *you can buy more stuff.*

But prices also have macroeconomic content. The prices of movie tickets and petrol and everything in an economy may change with respect to the euro, based on changes in the supply of and demand for money in various forms. If demand to hold euros rises then other things equal the price of euros will rise, meaning that the price of everything else must fall. And a fall in the price level also means a fall in the income level (since one person's spending is another's income). People can't buy more stuff because there is less money circulating. And to the extent that prices don't adjust smoothly in response to these dynamics, resources get idled. Maybe a firm is confused into thinking that falling prices are a micro rather than a macro phenomenon and opts not to adjust its prices in response, or maybe the boss would like to adjust prices but is locked into labour or supplier contracts or doesn't want to anger workers. Whatever the nature of the rigidity, if there are fewer euros circulating and prices don't fall correspondingly, then inventory and workers that were previously being employed won't be any longer.

This is the situation in which the euro area finds itself. And so you have inflation running at a much lower pace than it did a year ago (1.4% on latest estimate versus 2.4% in May of 2012) *and* you have broad year-on-year declines in euro-area retail activity. With low inflation, euro-area residents find they can buy less stuff.

Now the bruising part of this is that euro-area economies might at least hope that with low inflation *other* people could buy more stuff. If low inflation in Spain were matched by high inflation in Germany, then Spanish products and workers would look steadily more attractive to German households and firms. That is a raw deal for Spaniards, but it is one in which Spanish employment should stabilise and recover. One could potentially paraphrase Mr Draghi's statement as: with low inflation, Germans can buy more stuff.

But Mr Draghi sets monetary policy for the euro area as a whole, and he has not seen fit to encourage more euro-area-wide inflation. (Thus the pleading of the questioner in the quote above.) And that's very bad. Given the increasing salience of price and wage rigidities at very low inflation rates, the choice of a low *euro-wide* rate effectively compresses the north-south inflation differential, making life much harder for unemployed Spaniards and Italians. Rubbing salt in the wounds, Mr Draghi's very next words were:

Second, we don't see deflation and that is what we have to fear. We don't see that yet.

Core prices in Greece fell 2.0% in the year to April, according to Eurostat. A shame Mr Draghi didn't see that.

The euro crisis

Leaving the debts behind
Jun 12th 2013, 14:58 by R.A. | WASHINGTON

-
-

MATT YGLESIAS links to a piece updating us on the migratory solution to euro-zone unemployment:

A study by Real Instituto Elcano in February showed 70% of Spaniards under 30 have considered moving abroad. Portugal has seen 2% of its population leave in the past two years. The numbers leaving every year has doubled since 2008. A record 3,000 people are leaving Ireland every month, the highest level since the famine of the 19th-century. Some of them are Poles going home, but many of them are Irish.

Not surprisingly, a lot of them are moving to Germany. More than a million migrants moved to Germany last year, according to the Federal Statistics office, a rise of 13% from a year earlier. The number of immigrants coming from Spain, Greece, Portugal and Italy has risen by between 40% and 45% compared to 2012. But others are heading to wherever they have traditionally found work: Britain for the Irish, South America for the Spanish, and the U.S. for the Italians.

As Mr Yglesias notes, this is one of the shock-absorbing mechanisms euro-area pioneers envisioned, and it is certainly better for Spaniards to be working in Germany than doing nothing in Spain. But in the absence of a mechanism for debt mutualisation across the euro area, I worry about some of the knock-on effects of large-scale migration.

Labour is one of the main inputs to growth, and a reduction in the size of the underlying labour force through migration will shrink potential output across the periphery, making existing debt loads harder to bear. This could be especially bad if young workers are the ones leaving. That would worsen the dependency ratio as well; there would be fewer potential taxpayers in Spain and Italy to pay for the benefits flowing to a rapidly growing population of pensioners. The greater these migratory flows, the worse the fiscal outlook for the periphery.

To some extent, remittance flows could help. But a greater reliance on migration as a solution to the euro area's macroeconomic difficulties could *increase* rather than reduce demands for deeper fiscal integration.

The euro crisis

A delicate proposal
Jun 26th 2012, 19:32 by Charlemagne | BRUSSELS

- •
- •

HOW TO resolve the euro's woes? Angela Merkel says Germany will not agree to pool sovereign debt or share banking liabilities with other countries until there is greater political union. François Hollande says France cannot accept the loss of sovereignty without greater solidarity. So today Herman Van Rompuy, the president of the European Council (who chairs European summits), issued a report that tries to split the difference: there should be both joint liabilities and more European-level control of national policies.
Drafted with three others—José Manuel Barroso, president of the European Commission, Mario

Draghi, president of the European Central Bank, and Jean-Claude Juncker, president of the

Eurogroup (made up of finance ministers of the euro zone)—the report is thus a delicate piece of diplomacy at a time of sharp differences between Germany and France; indeed between Germany and many of the euro zone's biggest countries.

It sets out four "building blocks" for deeper euro-zone integration: a European system to guarantee bank deposits and manage troubled banks; fiscal integration to exert greater control on national budgets and steps towards issuing joint debt; more integration in economic policy-making to boost competitiveness; and more democratic accountability in European-level decisions. Precisely what these building blocks consist of, how the steps should be sequenced and how much can be done within existing treaties is all left a bit vague. The paper is peppered with words like "appropriate" and "commensurate" without attempting to define them.

On what many in Brussels call "banking union", it proposes creating a fund, "primarily funded" through contributions from banks, to help guarantee deposits and wind up failed banks. To be credible the fund should be backstopped by the euro zone's permanent rescue fund, the European Stability Mechanism (ESM), expected to be activated in the coming weeks.

On fiscal union, the report goes beyond the current system of euro-zone controls on national budget. It suggests jointly setting the ceiling for each country's debt and deficit. Governments would have to seek permission to break these limits, and Brussels could demand changes. Greater budget controls could, later on, lead to some form of Eurobonds (or "Eurobills" for short-dated debt). This is how the report puts the delicate issue:

In a medium term perspective, the issuance of common debt could be explored as an element of such a fiscal union and subject to progress on fiscal integration. Steps towards the introduction of joint and several sovereign liabilities could be considered as long as a robust framework for budgetary discipline and competitiveness is in place to avoid moral hazard and foster responsibility and compliance. The process towards the issuance of common debt should be criteria-based and phased, whereby progress in the pooling of decisions on budgets would be accompanied with commensurate steps towards the pooling of risks. Several options for partial common debt issuance have been proposed, such as the pooling of some short-term funding instruments on a limited and conditional basis, or the gradual roll-over into a redemption fund. Different forms of fiscal solidarity could also be envisaged.

Even further in the future, the euro zone could create a common treasury with some kind of central budget.

The report has been toned down in drafting, and some contentious ideas have been dropped. Gone is the call, made in an earlier version, for an "immediate and permanent" mutualisation of risk to backstop the banking sector. Ditto for the idea that the ESM could recapitalise banks directly (so relieving some troubled sovereigns like Spain from having to take on a big additional debt burden). The report is also silent on the question of a financial-transactions tax, no doubt to avoid upsetting a British government that is wary of stronger European bank supervision.

It is worth comparing the wooliness of Mr Van Rompuy's paper with the detail of the more convincingly worked-out proposal (here) issued on the same day by a group of prominent economists under the aegis of Jacques Delors, the former commission president, and Helmut Schmidt, the former German chancellor. It calls, for instance, for the creation of a special fund to help countries weather cyclical downturns. It also proposes a European debt agency to oversee the issuance of limited amounts of joint Eurobonds (typically up to 10% of GDP, with more possible if a country is willing to cede ever more budgetary decision-making powers).

Mr Van Rompuy's report does not pretend to be a "roadmap" to greater fiscal federalism. It is, instead, a proposal to talk about one. European officials argue that just getting Mrs Merkel to agree in principle to discuss things like the mutualisation of debt would be a big achievement, as would getting the French to talk about surrendering the powers of the Fifth Republic. Yet talking is one thing, agreeing quite another—and there is still no sign of accord among leaders.

Mr Van Rompuy says a detailed plan for integration could be presented in December, with perhaps an interim version issued in October. But will the markets be ready to wait that long? After all, this is the week that Cyprus asked for a bail-out, and Spain confirmed it would seek up to €100 billion to recapitalise its banks.

The likelihood is that this week's European summit will disappoint, and that could set off another round of panic in the markets. If the euro is to survive, Mr Van Rompuy may have to draft his roadmap rather sooner than he expects.

The euro crisis

Europe bleeds out

Apr 30th 2013, 14:27 by R.A. | WASHINGTON

-
-

IT IS a car crash of a data release. One simply can't look away. Hard to know precisely which part of the euro area's latest unemployment report is the most grimly compelling. The overall rate, at 12.1%? In the spring of 2010 unemployment rates in America and the euro zone were effectively the same at about 10%. There is now a gap of 4.5 percentage points. Total unemployment? In the first three years of the downturn America did far worse than the euro area, adding some 7.5m workers to the unemployment rolls to Europe's 4.7m. Since then total unemployment in the euro area has risen by another 3.2m while America reduced the ranks of the jobless by 3.5m. The euro area now has some 19.2m unemployed workers.

Individual country numbers inspire their own brand of horror. Greek joblessness topped 27% in

January (the most recent month for which data there are available), while Spanish employment has

risen to 26.7%. Joblessness in France rose by slightly more in the year to March than it did in Italy.

And did you know that Dutch unemployment rose by 1.4 percentage points over the past year?

German unemployment, of course, has held steady at 5.4% since last summer.

It is the youth figures that are most remarkable, however: 59.1% of those under 25 are unemployed in

Greece, 55.9% in Spain, 38.4% in Italy, 38.3% in Portugal, 26.5% in France—3.6m youths in all.

There is blame to go around for this, but one has to reserve special criticism for the European Central

Bank. The Federal Reserve's main policy rate has been effectively zero since late 2008; the ECB's

has never fallen below the current 0.75% level. The Fed has undertaken major asset-purchase

programmes in an effort to raise growth expectations, lower interest rates, and improve lending

conditions; the ECB deployed a special lending programme to banks last year in order to prevent a

systemic collapse, but its balance sheet has since been shrinking as those loans are repaid. The Fed

has reacted to weakening inflation and inflation expectations and has linked policy changes to labour

market indicators. The ECB has presided over a wrenching disinflation that has brought inflation

well below target, and which is both a consequence of recession and itself an implement of macroeconomic pain. Europe's governments have behaved badly, but American fiscal policy has hardly been better. The ECB faces a more complicated set of political constraints, but it has already proven how adroitly, aggressively, and inventively it can act when necessary.

The ECB meets this week. On Thursday it may announce an interest-rate cut; if it doesn't it is probable that a cut will be made in June. But a rate cut will not be enough, not remotely. As things stand ECB policy is scarcely being transmitted to the periphery, where rates to firms and households are far higher than in Germany. The euro area needs a jolt to expectations, targeted credit easing designed to improve peripheral liquidity, and broad quantitative easing. Mario Draghi has surprised markets before. Hopefully he will do so again. Because at the moment, the ECB is behaving as though the main economic failure in the 1930s was the world's pathetic inability to grit its teeth and endure the costs of tight money.

Add Hollandaise sauce

TEN YEARS ago Romano Prodi, the-then president of the European Commission, created a stink when he declared that the euro zone's budget rules were "stupid" because they were too rigid. But with the onset of the euro zone's debt crisis in 2010 the response has been to try to make them even stiffer.

At Germany's insistence, the euro zone first gave the commission more powers to monitor and enforce deficit limits, including the threat of "semi-automatic" sanctions for rule-breakers. And second, almost all members of the European Union were dragooned into signing up to the fiscal compact, a new treaty requiring then to adopt binding balanced-budget rules, preferably in their constitutions.

The election of a Socialist, François Hollande, as France's new president, is causing a rethink in Brussels. There is certainly a change of rhetoric about a "growth compact". But in substance, the change may be rather modest.

To begin with, Germany says the text of the fiscal compact is non-negotiable, a position that Mr Hollande's lieutenants seem to understand. Instead they want some form of programme to promote growth to be created alongside. Whether this takes the form of a formal protocol attached to the treaty (which must also be ratified), or a looser agreement, is yet to be decided. But with parts of Europe back in recession, leaders agree that they have to be seen to do more to promote growth.
In truth, the idea of growth was never absent from the European response to the crisis. Summits have been debating the issue since January. But fundamentally, in the view of Germany (adopted in large measure by the commission) growth would come firstly from restoring market confidence, by getting a grip on public finances. And secondly it would come from supply-side structural reforms to make countries more competitive and labour markets more flexible. With the rise of Mr Hollande, there is now a greater focus on boosting demand as well.
Although he belongs to the European People's Party, the same centre-right political grouping as France's defeated President Nicolas Sarkozy, the current commission president, José Manuel Barroso, warmly embraced Mr Hollande and his call for growth. "I am extremely pleased to see the new momentum that is clearly building in our member states to kick-start the stalled engine of growth," he said at a press conference today.
Far from being stupid, says Mr Barroso, the euro zone's budget rules are intelligent, because they allow for "adaptability" - though precisely how they can to be adapted remains to be seen (more on this below).
Mr Barroso was careful to say there should be no let-up in deficit-cutting, let alone a splurge of public spending. "Debt-fuelled growth is unsustainable", he insisted, adding that Mr Hollande emphasised his commitment to bringing down France's deficit.
So what to do about growth if there is little or no more money available? One proposal is to recapitalise the European Investment Bank (EIB), which has started to cut back on lending for fear of losing its credit rating.

Another is to leverage uncommitted bits of the EU's budget, in collaboration with the EIB, to raise new joint "project bonds" to finance new infrastructure projects. A modest sum of €230m could generate €4.6 billion worth of projects, says the Commission. It argues that such investments, for things like trans-national electricity grids and pipelines, would not take place if left to member-states. These ideas are sensible. Channelling the funds through the EIB, provides some assurance that the projects make economic sense and are managed properly. But even if countries agree to provide the EIB with the extra €10 billion that the commission is calling for, nobody should think that such extra money will lift the most troubled parts of the euro zone out of their recession.

There is a danger, moreover, of assuming that just because some European-level investment can be of benefit, all European spending must by definition be good. Sadly, this is what the commission is doing when seized the moment to urge members to support its demand for an enlarged EU budget, both for next year and for the seven-year period starting in 2014. "It will be a contradiction to support growth through investment and not be able to commit the funds necessary to work for that at the European level," declared Mr Barroso.

It is not, surely, a contradiction to point out that an organisation that still spends about four-tenths of its budget on agricultural subsidies is failing to make the best economic investments.

The commission's proposals are not new, but it is pleased that Mr Hollande has already made them his own and hopes he will champion them. "We are seizing the moment to advance our previous proposals in the new political climate," said Olli Rehn, the economic and monetary affairs commissioner.

The novelty may come in the coming days. The European Commission is in the final throes of debating proposals to relax the deficit-cutting targets. The IMF has made clear its view that the adjustment in European countries has often proven to be too harsh. Its latest work on the effect of fiscal consolidation finds that, in a downturn, deficit-cuttting has a strong multiplier effect that pushes countries into unexpectedly deep recession.

Mario Monti, Italy's prime minister, does not seem to have made much headway in his call for spending on "investment" to be excluded, wholly or partly, from the reckoning of a country's deficit. Instead, the Commission may agree to give some countries more time to get their deficits below 3% of GDP, the threshold set by the euro's original Stability and Growth Pact. This is what Mr Rehn had to say in a speech on April 5th:

Contrary to the misleading impression promoted by some politicians and pundits that the EU fiscal framework forces all member states into a 'one-size-fits-all' consolidation straightjacket, the Stability and Growth Pact is not stupid. Yes, the EU fiscal framework is rules-based, with clear reference values for public deficit and debt for triggering the excessive deficit procedure and, if needed, sanctions. But, at the same time, the Pact entails considerable scope for judgement, based on economic analysis and its legal provisions, when it comes to its application. The Pact underlines the structural sustainability of public finances over the medium term and implies differentiation among the member states according to their fiscal space and macroeconomic conditions.

All this verbiage probably spells "less pain in Spain". Last year it posted a deficit of 8.5% of GDP, substantially higher than its target of 6%. It has been allowed to overshoot its target this year, on condition that it keeps its promise to get the deficit below 3% of GDP next year. Though it is not officially asking for a reprieve, Spain may be granted an extra year to make the target.

An obvious time to announce the change could be Friday May 11th, when the commission is due to issue its spring economic forecast (which will then form the basis of detailed "country-specific" recommendations at the end of the month).

That said, the commission wants to see greater evidence that Spain is making the full effort to control public finances. It wants to see the budget cuts that Spain has promised this year, and evidence that Madrid is getting a grip on spending in the regions. The commission also wants Spain to draw up a convincing plan to stabilise its troubled banks. Moreover, the commission may push Spain to commit to a two-yearly budget cycle to provide greater clarity. "The road to medium-term economic sustainability goes through immediate decisive action in structural reforms and financial stability," said Mr Rehn.

Any move to lengthen the process of bringing down the deficit will have to be weighed against two factors. First is the impact on the markets: will investors fear that such a move heralds the breakdown of fiscal discipline, or rejoice that recession might be less deep? And how to explain the favour done to Spain to other countries, such as Belgium, that were told to cut the budget more deeply to meet their target, or face sanctions?

Whatever the "Hollande effect" on European policy towards public finances, the new French president is likely to be confronted with an uncomfortable decision. The commission's economic forecast is likely to find that, on current policies, France is likely to miss its 3% target next year (the IMF reckons the deficit will be 3.9%). So even before he is formally installed as president, Mr Hollande may be asked to spell out how he intends to keep his promises both to control debt and to relieve Europe of the curse of austerity. Unlike Spain, France is unlikely to get a deadline extension.: it cannot claim to have done everything possible to control the deficit, or that it is the victim of an unexpectedly severe recession.

Europe's budgetary policy may be getting a dollop of Hollandaise sauce, but beneath it all it will still be the same austere dish.